PRACTICE MAKES PERFECT

English Grammar for ESL Learners

ANSWERS

A.

1.   John works hard, **and/ so** he may win a scholarship.

2.   Bruce works just as hard, but/ yet he probably won't win anything.

3.   The doctor did her best, and/ so she saved the patient's life.

4.   The doctor did her best, but/ yet she couldn't save the patient's life.

5.   I plan on leaving early, so I need to get up at 5:00 a.m.

6.   This is a difficult book, and/ so it requires a great deal of concentration to read.

B.

1.   **When** Michael drinks beer, he gets a headache.
     OR
     Michael gets a headache **when** he drinks beer. (The subordinating conjunctions "because," "after," "once," "if," and "as soon as" could also be used.)

2.   **Because** she studies hard, she should pass the test.
     OR
     She should pass the test **because** she studies hard.
     ("Since," "provided," and "once" could also be used.)

3.   **Although** I enjoy tennis, I haven't played in a year.
     OR
     I haven't played in a year **although** I enjoy tennis.

4.   **Until** the mover arrived, he decided to do nothing.
     OR
     He decided to do nothing **until** the mover arrived.

5.   **After** the maid served dinner, she left for the day.
     OR
     The maid left for the day **after** she served dinner.
     ("Before," "when," "as soon as," and "once" could also be used.)

6.   **Before** he mailed the letter, he put on the stamp.
     OR
     He put on the stamp **before** he mailed the letter.

7.   **As soon as** the new law is enacted, income taxes will increase by 30 percent.
     OR
     Income taxes will increase by 30 percent **as soon as** the new law is enacted.
     ("When," "after," "once," and "provided that" could also be used.)

8.   **If** you like it, you can have it.
     OR
     You can have it **if** you like it.

12

C.

1. Bruce is lazy. Ralph and his sister are no better.

2. It's a good thing you're friends with him. He's awfully cruel to his enemies.

3. He knew the right thing to do. That makes no difference now.

4. I thought they considered me very funny. Therefore, I told another joke.

5. On his way to Alaska, he experienced many difficulties. After much hardship, he arrived at his destination.

6. The jolt threw me against the steering wheel. For a second, I lost all sense of time. Slowly I drifted into unconsciousness.

D.

1. Although I tried hard, I still failed.

2. While the cat's away, the mice will play.

3. Before you buy a car, check the tires.

4. Because he studies long hours, he should pass the course.

5. Since he knows the rules, he will do well at the game.

6. When you go swimming, take along a friend.

E.

1. Pete Rose, formerly of the Cincinnati Reds, is my hero.

2. The employees are not paid for overtime.

3. I have the ability to learn from my mistakes.

4. There is something I've been meaning to tell you.

PRACTICE
MAKES
PERFECT

English Grammar for ESL Learners

Ed Swick

McGraw·Hill

New York   Chicago   San Francisco   Lisbon   London   Madrid   Mexico City
Milan   New Delhi   San Juan   Seoul   Singapore   Sydney   Toronto

5 6 7 8 9 0   QPD/QPD   3 2 1 0 9 8 7

ISBN 0-07-144132-8
Library of Congress control number 2004112656

McGraw-Hill books are available at special quantity discounts to use as premiums and sales promotions, or for use in corporate training programs. For more information, please write to the Director of Special Sales, Professional Publishing, McGraw-Hill, Two Penn Plaza, New York, NY 10121-2298. Or contact your local bookstore.

This book is printed on acid-free paper.

Contents

Introduction		vii
Unit 1	**Nouns**	1
Unit 2	**Definite and Indefinite Articles**	6
Unit 3	**Adjectives**	9
Unit 4	**Personal Pronouns**	12
Unit 5	**Verbs**	17
Unit 6	**Auxiliary Verbs**	44
Unit 7	**Passive Voice**	49
Unit 8	**Subjunctive Mood**	53
Unit 9	**Adverbs**	59
Unit 10	**Contractions**	62
Unit 11	**Plurals**	65
Unit 12	**Punctuation**	68
Unit 13	**Infinitives and Gerunds**	75
Unit 14	**Relative Pronouns**	77
Unit 15	**Reflexive Pronouns**	83
Unit 16	**Possession**	86
Unit 17	**Possessive Pronouns**	88
Unit 18	**Prepositions**	92
Unit 19	**Capitalization**	95
Unit 20	**Comparative and Superlative Forms**	99
Unit 21	**Conjunctions**	106
Unit 22	**Interrogatives**	110

Unit 23   **Negation**   115

Unit 24   **Numbers**   120

Unit 25   **Some Important Contrasts**   125

Appendix: Common Irregular Verbs   133

Answer Key   135

Introduction

Many people consider learning grammar a chore. And at times, it can be. But understanding the grammar of any language is essential for becoming a skilled and accurate user of that language. English is certainly no exception.

The rules of grammar for a language learner are like the rules of the road for a driver. In order to be able to drive properly and maneuver with other drivers, you have to know the rules that everyone goes by. Naturally, some people break the rules and make driving difficult for other drivers. This is true of language, too. If you follow the rules of grammar, you can express yourself clearly. But if you fail to observe those rules, people may find it difficult to understand you or they may even misunderstand you entirely. So it's really very important to understand and use correct grammar.

But what is grammar? Funk and Wagnalls's *New College Standard Dictionary* describes grammar as "a type of science that explains the various principles of oral or written usage of a particular language." It is also said to be "the developed art of speaking or writing accurately in a particular language." Whether science or art, grammar is made up of the descriptions that tell you how to use a language correctly. For example:

> **Description:** Begin a sentence with *do* to change a statement to a question.
> **Usage:** Statement = "You understand the problem."
> Question = "*Do* you understand the problem?"

Or:

> **Description:** Use *he* as the subject of a sentence; use *him* as the direct object.
> **Usage:** Subject = "*He* is a good friend of mine."
> Direct Object = "I visit *him* very often."

There are many such grammatical descriptions, and each one is a building block in the structure of your knowledge of how to form and use English correctly. The greater the number of building blocks that you master, the greater your accuracy with the spoken and written language will be.

Standard grammar is composed of the traditional rules for English. It is what grammarians and English professors *want* everyone to use when they speak and write. But a language evolves over time, and the traditional rules sometimes seem out of step with what is going on in the English-speaking world. The more current or popular usages can be called *casual language*. That's what people really say in their everyday lives and is often in direct contradiction with standard grammar. As an illustration, in standard grammar you should use *who* as the subject of a sentence and use *whom* when it is used as an object. But that's not always the case in casual language. For example:

> **Standard grammar:** "*Whom* did you visit in New York?"
> **Casual language:** "*Who* did you visit in New York?"

Although the first example is considered better grammatically, the second example sentence is the most commonly used.

Another kind of example involves the verb *to dive*. Its past tense is either regular (*dived*) or irregular (*dove*). What is the difference? Essentially, none. Both forms are used correctly as the past tense. But English is evolving. Things are changing. And the English-speaking world is deciding whether it wants the past tense of the verb *to dive* to be regular or irregular. It may take quite a while longer to learn what that decision will be. So for the time being you'll continue to hear both *dived* and *dove* in the past tense.

There is a similar case with the verb *to prove*. Nowadays, many people use *proved* as the participle in a perfect tense: "He has proved" or "We had not proved." But there are others who still use the archaic form (*proven*), which today is generally accepted as an adjective, in place of *proved*: "He has proven" or "We had not proven."

The point here is that grammar rules will guide you toward speaking and writing better English. But many rules of grammar are broken by certain casual or popular usages and still others become unclear because the language is in a state of transition. Where these deviations occur, they will be discussed in this book, because if English learners only know that *who* should be used as a subject of a sentence, they will be confused by what occurs in casual language: "*Who* did you visit in New York?"

However, just knowing the rules of grammar is not enough. This book will also provide you with abundant practice in using English grammar. The more you practice, the more you become proficient in how you use English and to what extent you understand it. There are various kinds of exercises to allow you to manipulate the language from different angles. The Answer Key at the end of the book gives you not only the right answers but also suggestions as to how an exercise should be completed.

English grammar isn't necessarily a chore. Indeed, it can be your key to unlocking a very rich treasure.

Nouns

Nouns can be either *proper* or *common*. Proper nouns are those that refer to a *particular* person, place, thing, or idea. Such nouns are capitalized: *America, George Washington, Mr. Neruda, October.*

Nouns that do not refer to a particular person, place, thing, or idea are common nouns. They are not capitalized: *land, girls, money, test.* Compare the following list of proper and common nouns:

Proper Nouns	**Common Nouns**
Mexico	country
Ms. Finch	woman
English	language
McGraw-Hill	publisher
American Airlines	company
December	month

exercise | **1-1**

Next to each noun write the word proper *or* common.

1. _____ France

2. _____ rope

3. _____ United States

4. _____ Professor Hall

5. _____ professor

6. _____ the stadium

7. _____ the Olympics

8. _____ horses

9. _____ Dr. Blanchard

10. _____ our school

| exercise | 1-2 |

Rewrite each noun, capitalizing the proper nouns.

1. _____ glass

2. _____ rocky mountains

3. _____ mexico

4. _____ flowers

5. _____ bus

6. _____ the store

7. _____ new york times

8. _____ roberto

9. _____ professor romano

10. _____ my books

Nouns can be used as the *subject of a sentence*. The subject is the word that is performing the action in the sentence. The subject can be a proper noun or a common noun, and it can be singular or plural:

> *Juanita* is a friend of mine.
> *The boys* like to play soccer.
> Where is the *school*?

Nouns can also be used as *direct objects*. The direct object in a sentence is the noun that receives the action of the verb. To find the direct object in a sentence do three things:

1. Find the subject of the sentence.
2. Find the verb in the sentence.
3. Ask whom or what with the subject and the verb.

Look at these sample sentences:

"Sara likes my brother."

1. subject = *Sara*
2. verb = *likes*

"The girls find a book."

1. subject = *girls*
2. verb = *find*

3. ask whom = Whom does Sara like?	3. ask what = What do the girls find?
The direct object is *my brother*	The direct object is *book*.

Nouns are sometimes *indirect objects*. They stand before the direct object in the sentence. It is the person to whom or for whom something is provided. To find the indirect object in a sentence do three things:

1. Find the subject of the sentence.
2. Find the verb in the sentence.
3. Ask to whom or for whom with the subject and the verb.

Look at these sample sentences:

"Justin buys the girl a magazine."   "Mother gives Nate five dollars."

1. subject = *Justin*
2. verb = *buys*
3. ask to whom or for whom = For whom does Justin buy a magazine?

1. subject = *Mother*
2. verb = *gives*
3. ask to whom or for whom = To whom does Mother give five dollars?

The indirect object is *girl.*   The indirect object is *Nate.*

Note: It is rare that something inanimate is used as an indirect object.

When a noun is used as a *predicate noun*, it follows the predicate in the sentence. The predicate can be a single verb or a verb phrase:

Verb as the predicate: Maria *helps* us.
Verb phrase as the predicate: Maria *usually helps with the gardening.*

Predicate nouns most often follow the verbs *to be* and *to become*:

My mother wants to be *a doctor.*
Celine became *an actress.*
Are you *the manager* of this building?

exercise   1-3

Look at the italicized word in each sentence. Decide how it is used, then write subject, direct object, indirect object, *or* predicate noun *in the blank.*

1. _____ Claudia likes *Bret.*

2. _____ *The boys* found some money.

3. _____ The girls found *some money.*

4. _____ My father is *an engineer.*

5. _____ I sent *my sister* a telegram.

6. _____ Tomas buys *Serena* three red roses.

7. _____ Is *the woman* at home now?

8. _____ Mr. Jimenez became *a pilot.*

9. _____ He needs *a new car.*

10. _____ Carmen gives them *the books.*

exercise	1-4

Write a sentence using the noun given as a direct object.

> EXAMPLE: the boy
> *Barbara sees **the boy** in the park.*

1. my sister

   _____

2. a new car

   _____

3. Jackie

   _____

Write a sentence using the word given as an indirect object.

4. the children

   _____

5. a puppy

   _____

6. Grandfather

   _____

exercise	1-5

Using the phrase in parentheses, answer each question using that phrase as the direct or indirect object.

> EXAMPLE: (Yolanda) Whom does Gerry meet?
> *Gerry meets Yolanda.*

1. (the boys) Whom does the girl not trust?

   _____

2. (his wallet) What does Father often misplace?

   _____

3. (the landlord) To whom does she always give the rent money?

   _____

4. (her new computer) What does Anita want to sell soon?

   _____

5. (her grandchildren) For whom does she buy the toys?

   _____

6. (Ms. Johnson) Whom must you visit in New York?

   _____

7. (their new house) What do they like so much?

   _____

8. (little Johnny) To whom can she give the present?

   _____

9. (Dr. Lee) Whom does he need to see today?

   _____

10. (Michael) To whom does she throw the ball?

    _____

Definite and Indefinite Articles

The English **definite article** is *the*. It is used to identify a *particular* person or thing. If you are speaking about someone or something you are already familiar with, you use *the* with the noun. Look at these examples:

> I already know *the man*.
> She met *the women* who won the lottery.
> This is *the book* that I told you about.

The **indefinite article** is used to describe someone or something that is unfamiliar to you or about which you are speaking *in general*. There are two forms: *a* and *an*. Use *a* before a word beginning with a consonant. Use *an* before a word beginning with a vowel. Look at these examples:

> He sees *a stranger* on the corner.
> Did you buy *an apple* or *an orange*?
> Is the woman *a good lawyer*?
> She has *an idea*.

Compare the difference between the definite and indefinite article by using these sentences:

> I want *an* apple. (I do not see an apple. But I feel hungry for one.)

> I want *the* apple. (I am choosing between the apple and the orange that I see before me.)

The definite article for plural nouns is also *the*. But there is no indefinite article for plural nouns. The plural articles are used in the same way as the singular articles.

Singular Definite	Singular Indefinite	Plural Definite	Plural Indefinite
the boy	a boy	the boys	boys
the house	a house	the houses	houses
the idea	an idea	the ideas	ideas

exercise   2-1

Fill in the blank with either the definite or indefinite article, whichever makes the best sense.

1. Did you buy a Ford or _____ Chevy?

2. Does he know _____ man on the corner?

3. She has _____ secret to tell you.

4. What time does _____ train leave?

5. We need _____ hot dogs and a bottle of Coke.

6. Did you see _____ accident?

7. He met _____ guests as they arrived.

8. _____ teacher is angry with us.

9. I can't find _____ keys.

10. Is that _____ snake in that tree?

exercise   2-2

Rewrite each sentence, changing the singular nouns in each sentence to plural nouns. Make any changes to the articles and verbs that are necessary.

1. They gave us an orange.

   _____

2. I like the book very much.

   _____

3. Do you often visit the farm there?

   _____

4. A rabbit is hiding behind it.

    _____

5. Katrina likes to play with the kitten.

    _____

Follow the same directions, but change the plural nouns to singular.

6. Montel has dogs and cats.

    _____

7. I want to buy the roses.

    _____

8. There are gifts for you.

    _____

9. Can you hear the babies crying?

    _____

10. Do you have brothers or sisters?

    _____

Adjectives are words that describe nouns. They tell the size, color, or quality of something: a *big* room, the *red* car, four *interesting* books. Here are some commonly used adjectives:

beautiful	fast	loud	tall
big	funny	old	terrible
black	handsome	quiet	thirsty
boring	interesting	right	ugly
careful	late	sad	young
careless	little	short	white
early	long	slow	wrong

exercise 3-1

Circle the adjective that makes more sense in the sentence.

1. I often go to a **green/late** movie.

2. Their **little/right** boy is six years old.

3. The **wrong/young** teacher is very smart.

4. We took the **fast/loose** train to New York.

5. The **old/funny** story made me laugh.

6. Do you know that **handsome/early** man?

7. She had an **early/careless** breakfast.

8. I saw the **long/terrible** accident.

9. The new house has **boring/white** doors.

10. The **green/short** boy is my cousin.

Just like nouns, adjectives can follow the predicate. They most often come after forms of the verbs *to be* and *to become*:

My sister was very *sad.*
The horse suddenly became *thirsty.*
My grandfather is *old.*

exercise	3-2

Look at the example sentences. Change each sentence so that the adjective follows the predicate.

EXAMPLE: The white house is on the hill.
The house on the hill is white.

1. The sad song was from Mexico.

   _____

2. The funny story is about a clown.

   _____

3. The careless waiter is out of work.

   _____

4. The ugly snake is from Egypt.

   _____

5. The beautiful woman is from Spain.

   _____

exercise	3-3

Fill in the blank with any adjective that makes sense. You may choose from the list given at the beginning of the unit.

1. David wrote a _____ poem for her.

2. Do you like the _____ cake?

3. I cannot find an _____ book.

4. Where does the _____ lawyer live?

5. Marisa needs a _____ job.

6. The _____ man found a _____ wallet.

7. Kareem is a _____ friend of mine.

8. There is a _____ test tomorrow.

9. When can you come to our _____ farm?

10. That is a _____ question.

Personal Pronouns

Pronouns are words that take the place of nouns. The English personal pronouns are:

	Singular	Plural
First Person	I	we
Second Person	you	you
Third Person	he, she, it	they

Notice that *you* is both singular and plural. When speaking to one person, say *you*. When speaking to two or more persons, say *you*:

Tim, *you* are a very good student.
Bruno and Rene, *you* have to study more.

Just as nouns have gender, pronouns also do. *I*, *we*, and *you* can be used by males or females. *He* is always masculine, *she* is always feminine, and *it* is always neuter. The plural of the third-person pronouns is always *they*, whether masculine, feminine, or neuter. And just like nouns, pronouns can be used as:

1. the subject of a sentence
2. a direct object
3. an indirect object

But when used as a direct object or indirect object, some of the pronouns change:

Subject	Direct Object	Indirect Object
I	me	me
you	you	you
he	him	him
she	her	her
it	it	it
we	us	us
you (plural)	you	you
they	them	them

If a pronoun replaces a noun in the sentence, it must have the same characteristics as the noun: the same number (singular or plural), the same gender (masculine, feminine, or neuter), and the same use in the sentence (subject, direct object, or indirect object). Look at these examples where the pronoun replaces the italicized noun:

Joseph is a hard worker. → *He* is a hard worker.
(singular masculine noun/subject) (singular masculine pronoun/subject)

Do you know *the girls*? → Do you know *them*?
(plural noun/direct object) (plural pronoun/direct object)

We gave *Mrs. Jones* some flowers. → We gave *her* some flowers.
(singular feminine noun/ (singular feminine pronoun/
indirect object) indirect object)

Notice that the nouns and pronouns are in the third person. This is true when a pronoun replaces a noun. But when a noun or pronoun is combined with the first-person singular pronoun *I*, it is replaced by the first-person plural pronoun *we*:

You and I have work to do. → *We* have work to do.
He helps *the girls and me.* → He helps *us*.

exercise 4-1

Look at the pronoun given in parentheses. Fill in the blank in the sentence with its correct form.

1. (you) How are _____ today?

2. (he) Caleb gave _____ a gift.

3. (she) _____ lives on Main Street.

4. (it) I really don't like _____.

5. (I) She met _____ in the city.

6. (Kris and I) Please give _____ the magazines.

7. (you and I) _____ worked in the garden.

8. (they) Are _____ your friends?

9. (we) The puppy followed _____ home.

10. (they) My brother saw _____ in New York.

11. (you) Mikhail wants to visit _____ today.

12. (I) When can _____ move into the apartment?

13. (it) Derrick bought _____ in Mexico.

14. (you and I) The children are helping _____ .

15. (she) I like _____ a lot.

exercise   4-2

Change the italicized noun in each sentence to the corresponding pronoun.

1. *The students* came to class late. _____

2. I found *the money* in the closet. _____

3. Her brother sent *Jennifer and me* a postcard. _____

4. Do *your parents* live in Florida? _____

5. *My landlady* is very nice. _____

6. Do you know *my landlady?* _____

7. *Boys* can get so dirty. _____

8. Did you lose *your wallet?* _____

9. Juan visits *his uncle* often. _____

10. May I borrow *your watch?* _____

exercise   4-3

Change the italicized pronoun in each sentence to any appropriate noun.

1. *We* often speak English. _____

2. Do you like *it?* _____

3. Where did you find *them?* _____

4. *She* is from Puerto Rico. _____

5. Patricia never met *him* before. _____

6. Is *he* sick today? _____

7. We sent *them* a box of candy. _____

8. *It* costs twenty dollars. _____

9. The boys watched *her*. _____

10. Do *they* understand us? _____

When you change a direct object noun to a direct object pronoun, you must add *to* or *for* before the indirect object noun or pronoun. The indirect object becomes the object of the preposition *to* or *for*. Place the prepositional phrase after the direct object. For example:

I gave Jay **a book**. → I gave **it** to Jay.
We buy her **flowers**. → We buy **them** for her.

exercise   **4-4**

Rewrite each sentence, changing the italicized direct object to a pronoun. Add to *or* for *appropriately.*

1. I sent my friends *a letter*.

  _____

2. She is giving us *two cakes*.

  _____

3. Trey sold her *his car*.

  _____

4. I didn't buy Ella *the scarf*.

  _____

5. My brother will bring me *my gloves*.

  _____

Nouns or pronouns can be used to complete *a prepositional phrase*. That is a phrase made up of a preposition and a noun or a pronoun. Here are some of the most commonly used prepositions:

after, behind, between, for, from, in, near, on, of, through, to, with, without

Look at these sample prepositional phrases:

after the concert	behind me
between the girls	for you
from a friend	in him
near the city	on it
of a book	through her
to a student	with us
without the money	without them

In a prepositional phrase, use the same form of the pronoun that is used as a direct or indirect object:

Subject Pronoun	Direct or Indirect Object	Prepositional Phrase
I	me	after me
you	you	behind you
he	him	for him
she	her	from her
it	it	in it
we	us	between us
they	them	near them

exercise 4-5

Complete the sentences changing the subject pronoun in parentheses to an object pronoun.

1. (I) They have a gift for _____.

2. (you) I sent some flowers to _____.

3. (he) Karen often comes home without _____.

4. (she) I like dancing with _____.

5. (it) We found something in _____.

6. (we) Teresa sits near _____.

7. (they) This is a letter from _____.

8. (Dwayne and I) He is speaking of _____.

9. (you and I) Someone is standing behind _____.

10. (he) You can come in after _____.

exercise 4-6

Change the italicized noun to a pronoun.

1. We are driving through *the tunnel.* _____

2. A wolf was standing between *the boys.* _____

3. Do you want to ride in *my car?* _____

4. The guests have something for *Julia.* _____

5. I like singing with *Mr. Garcia.* _____

6. Maria is sitting near *Ali and me.* _____

7. I get postcards from *the tourists.* _____

Verbs

Verbs are the words in a sentence that describe the action of a sentence or that introduce the condition or state of someone or something in the sentence.

Action: Anna *throws* the ball.

Introduction of a condition: Trent *is* very sick.

There are many *action verbs*. Those that can have a direct object are often called *transitive verbs*. Here is a list of some commonly used transitive verbs. Note that they can be used with a direct object.

Transitive Verbs	Used in a Sentence
buy	He buys a newspaper.
carry	I am carrying the child.
find	Can you find the book?
help	She helps us.
like	I don't like cabbage.
lose	Don't lose your money.
read	She is reading a book.
pull	The dentist pulled the tooth.
push	The boy pushes the cart.
sell	I am selling my car.
speak	Father speaks Spanish.
write	We are writing some postcards.
understand	Do you understand me?

Intransitive verbs are not followed by a direct object. They often show a movement to a place and are sometimes followed by a prepositional phrase. Following is a list of some commonly used intransitive verbs:

Intransitive Verbs	Used in a Sentence
come	Can you come to the party?
crawl	The baby crawls on the floor.
drive	We are driving fast.
fly	I flew here from Paris.
go	Are you going home?
hurry	We hurry to the window.
jump	Peter jumps from the roof.
ride	I am riding in his car.
run	The girls run past the school.
sail	We are sailing to Europe.
travel	Do you want to travel with us?
walk	I walk out of the theater.

Still other verbs introduce the condition or state of someone or something. They do not take a direct object and are most often followed by an adjective. These verbs are usually called *linking verbs*. Here are some commonly used linking verbs:

Linking Verbs	Used in a Sentence
appear	The boy appears quite well.
be	I am hungry.
become	The weather becomes bad.
feel	It feels hot.
grow	The dog is growing weak.
look	She looks unhappy.
seem	The coat seems too small for you.
smell	The pizza smells good.
sound	The music sounds awful.
taste	The popcorn tastes salty.

Careful! Some of the linking verbs have a second usage. They can be used as transitive verbs. Look at these examples:

> **Linking Verb:** His skin feels *hot.* (*hot* = adjective)
> **Transitive Verb:** He feels *a sharp pain.* (*a sharp pain* = direct object)

> **Linking Verb:** The sky grows *cloudy.* (adjective)
> **Transitive Verb:** We grow *vegetables.* (direct object)

> **Linking Verb:** That smells *beautiful.* (adjective)
> **Transitive Verb:** She smells *the flowers.* (direct object)

> **Linking Verb:** My coffee tastes *bitter.* (adjective)
> **Transitive Verb:** Risa tasted *the ice cream.* (direct object)

You can identify linking verbs by substituting *am, is,* or *are* for the verb. If the sentence makes sense with the substitution, it is a linking verb. If it does not make sense, it is a transitive verb. Some examples:

> It feels cold. (It *is* cold.) *This makes sense.* = Linking Verb
> He feels her pulse. (He *is* her pulse.) *This makes no sense.* = Transitive Verb

They smell nice. (They *are* nice.) *This makes sense.* = Linking Verb
We smell coffee. (We *are* coffee.) *This makes no sense.* = Transitive Verb

exercise	5-1

Look at the verb in each sentence. Decide what kind of verb it is. Then write transitive, intransitive, *or* linking *in the space provided.*

1. _____ Kirsten asks a good question.

2. _____ We went to Mexico.

3. _____ Do you understand German?

4. _____ It grows very dark.

5. _____ Emily appears healthy again.

6. _____ Mother bought a new car.

7. _____ The cat jumps from the sofa to the chair.

8. _____ Do they want tickets for the movie?

9. _____ The milk is too hot.

10. _____ Grandfather grows corn and potatoes in his garden.

The Present Tense

In some languages, present tense conjugations are very complicated. Each pronoun requires a different ending on the verb. English is much simpler. Only the third-person singular (he, she, it) requires an ending. That ending is an *-s* (or *-es*). And with some verbs there is no ending change at all. Look at these examples of the present tense:

	to go	**to see**	**to want**	**can**	**must**
I	go	see	want	can	must
you	go	see	want	can	must
he, she, it	goes	sees	wants	can	must
we	go	see	want	can	must
they	go	see	want	can	must

When the verb ends in the vowel *-o*, add *-es* for the third-person singular pronouns:

do → does

Can and *must* are special auxiliary verbs. They never have an ending change in the present tense. There are other auxiliaries that do the same thing. They will be taken up later.

exercise   5-2

Rewrite each sentence with the pronouns shown.

1. I rarely find a good book.

   You _____

   He _____

2. We often make mistakes.

   She _____

   They _____

3. He goes home early.

   We _____

   I _____

4. It can help us.

   They _____

   He _____

5. Randy and Kim do the dishes.

   She _____

   You _____

6. I must work tomorrow.

   They _____

   He _____

7. They borrow some money.

   I _____

   She _____

8. He sends a few postcards.

   You _____

   We _____

9. You can spend the night here.

   He _____

   They _____

10. It grows very slowly.

    They _____

    He _____

There are two special verbs that have more complicated ending changes in the present tense: *to have* and *to be*.

	to have	to be
I	have	am
you	have	are
he, she, it	has	is
we	have	are
they	have	are

exercise 5-3

Rewrite each sentence with the pronouns shown.

1. They have no money.

    She _____

    We _____

2. Mario is my cousin.

    He _____

    You _____

3. The boys are very sick.

    I _____

    She _____

4. His father has a new car.

    They _____

    He _____

5. I am at home now.

    They _____

    She _____

6. She is quite well.

    I _____

    He _____

7. He has no tickets.

They _____

She _____

8. We have a new apartment.

You _____

He _____

9. They are from Costa Rica.

He _____

I _____

10. I have a big problem.

They _____

She _____

exercise   5-4

Circle the boldface word that best completes each sentence.

1. They **goes/have** no time today.

2. My aunt **can/lives** in New York.

3. **She/They** speaks English and Spanish.

4. We **are/am** Americans.

5. **You/It** is in the city.

6. I **must/am** not a citizen.

7. **Are/Have** you at home now?

8. He **has/have** a new job.

9. She **likes/see** her neighbors.

10. **You/She** goes to the store.

Asking Questions

A sentence that has the verb *to be* in it is easily formed as a question. Just invert the position of the verb and the subject. Look at these examples:

Statement	Question
I am late.	Am I late?
She is his sister.	Is she his sister?
They are from Puerto Rico.	Are they from Puerto Rico?

All other verbs, including *to have*, form a question by using the verb *to do* (*do*, *does*). The verb *to do* is conjugated for the subject of the sentence. The original verb in the sentence becomes an infinitive. English infinitives begin with the word *to*: *to run, to jump, to sing*, and so on. Sometimes the word *to* is omitted: run, jump, sing, and so on. The word *to* is omitted in questions.

Statement	Question
Jacques has a new job.	Does Jacques have a new job?
You see the ocean.	Do you see the ocean?
She likes my brother.	Does she like my brother?
Tanya usually finds the books.	Does Tanya usually find the books?

exercise   5-5

Change each sentence to a question.

1. Rocco's uncle lives in Washington.

   _____

2. She is his cousin.

   _____

3. We take this road to Chicago.

   _____

4. They are in the garden.

   _____

5. I have your new address.

   _____

6. I am your student.

   _____

7. Linda likes Jack.

   _____

8. You buy flowers every day.

   _____

9. She sings beautifully.

   _____

10. It is a nice day.

   _____

exercise   5-6

Change each question to a statement.

1. Are the boys at home?

   _____

2. Do you want this book?

   _____

3. Does she have the money?

   _____

4. Am I your friend now?

   _____

5. Does he go there every day?

   _____

6. Is it in there?

   _____

7. Do you understand English?

   _____

8. Does the boy feel better?

   _____

9. Are you in the garden?

   _____

10. Do we have enough money?

   _____

Negation

Add *not* after the verb *to be* to make it negative:

> I am → I am not
> you are → you are not
> she is → she is not
> we are → we are not
> they are → they are not

With all other verbs, use *do/does* and *not* to make a verb negative. *Do* is conjugated for the subject of the sentence, and the original verb becomes an infinitive. The structure is *do + not + infinitive*. Look at these examples:

Original Sentence	Negative Sentence
I like hot milk.	I do not like hot milk.
She has my books.	She does not have my books.
Danielle goes to the window.	Danielle does not go to the window.
We find the money.	We do not find the money.
It grows cold.	It does not grow cold.

exercise   5-7

Negate each sentence by adding not *to it.*

1. Delores is in the capital.

   _____

2. We have enough money now.

   _____

3. My father sends him a postcard.

   _____

4. The books are on the table.

   _____

5. I go home late.

   _____

6. I am an American.

   _____

7. The girls buy some ice cream.

   _____

8. We do our homework.

   _____

9. Lisa likes my cousin.

   _____

10. It seems very old.

    _____

When a negative sentence becomes a question, the question begins with *do/does* as described earlier:

> you do not know → do you not know?
> Mary does not have → does Mary not have?

Even when negated, the verb *to be* does **not** form a question with *do/does*:

> I am not → am I not?
> she is not → is she not?
> they are not → are they not?

Some example sentences:

Negative Sentence	**Negative Question**
She does not like him.	Does she not like him?
We do not want it.	Do we not want it?
You are not at home.	Are you not at home?
He is not our friend.	Is he not our friend?

exercise 5-8

Rewrite each negative sentence as a negative question.

1. You do not have the time.

   _____

2. Mike does not like this book.

   _____

3. Kent is not at home.

   _____

4. He does not go there every day.

   _____

5. The girls are not happy.

   _____

6. Sean does not speak Spanish.

   _____

7. The boys do not make a cake for her.

   _____

8. They do not do this very often.

   _____

9. Mother does not have enough money.

   _____

10. I am not happy about it.

   _____

Three Forms of the Present Tense

English has three ways of expressing the present tense. You already know one way: Conjugate the verb by adding appropriate endings: *I sing, we go, he has, she is, they want, Toni finds*. This formation of the present tense has a special meaning. It says that someone does something as a habit or frequently.

The second present tense is formed from the verb *to be* combined with a verb ending in *-ing*: *I am running, you are speaking, she is learning, we are singing*, and so on. This present tense formation means that an action is in progress and that the action of the verb is incomplete.

The third present tense is the emphatic and opposite response to someone's statement. If the statement is negative, you respond in the positive. If it is positive, you respond in the negative. It requires using *do/does* with the infinitive of the original verb. Kendra says, "You do not have the book." You respond, "I *do* have the book." Scott says, "He does not go by bus." You respond, "He *does* go by bus." Sophie says, "My sister likes the movie." You respond, "Your sister *does not* like the movie."

Let's compare the three forms:

Habitual Statement (something done frequently)
I speak English.
We go to school.
They play soccer.

In Progress (incomplete)
I am speaking English.
We are going to school.
They are playing soccer.

Emphatic Response
"You do not speak English." → "I *do* speak English."
"We go to school." → "We *do not* go to school."
"They do not play soccer." → "They *do* play soccer."

When you use an adverb that shows that an action is done frequently (*often, sometimes, always, usually, every day*, etc.), you should use the habitual form of the present tense: *I often listen to jazz. We sometimes talk on the phone. Travis usually works until five.*

exercise   5-9

Rewrite each sentence using the adverb in parentheses. Change the verb action from being incomplete to habitual.

1. We are driving to New York. (always)

   _____

2. She is speaking quickly. (sometimes)

   _____

3. I am working in the garden. (often)

   _____

4. The boys are playing tennis. (frequently)

   _____

5. The women are traveling abroad. (every year)

   _____

6. Doug is buying German beer. (usually)

   _____

7. Michelle is talking on the phone. (always)

   _____

8. My brother is sleeping in the living room. (sometimes)

   _____

9. They are cooking a roast. (usually)

   _____

10. His sister is helping them. (every day)

   _____

exercise   **5-10**

Give an emphatic response to each statement.

> EXAMPLE: He does not speak English.
> *He does speak English.*

1. She does not understand the problem.

   _____

2. We go to the movies often.

   _____

3. I do not like that dress.

   _____

4. Mac wants to sell the old car.

   _____

5. Mr. Tyner writes him a long letter.

   _____

6. The boys do not work in this factory.

   _____

The Past Tense

The past tense is used to show something that has happened in the past. Just as there are three present tense formations, there are also three past tense formations: (1) a habitual or frequent action, (2) an action in progress or incomplete, and (3) an emphatic response in the past tense.

The past tense conjugation of a habitual or frequent action is quite simple. Just add *-ed* to the end of a regular verb. If the verb ends in a consonant followed by a *-y*, drop the *-y* and add *-ied*. If a one-syllable verb ends in a single consonant, double that consonant and add *-ed*. Look at these examples:

Just Add *-ed*	**Consonant *-y***	**Single Consonant**
borrow, borrowed	bury, buried	bed, bedded
call, called	carry, carried	pin, pinned
help, helped	hurry, hurried	rot, rotted
work, worked	rally, rallied	sin, sinned

The verbs listed above are *regular verbs*. They form their past tense by the addition of *-ed*. There are also *irregular verbs*. They form their past tense by making a change within the stem of the verb. It is usually a vowel change, but there can also be a consonant change as well. Following are the irregular past tense forms of some commonly used verbs:

Infinitive	Past Tense	Infinitive	Past Tense
to be	was/were	to make	made
to break	broke	to put	put
to bring	brought	to read	read
to build	built	to ride	rode
to buy	bought	to run	ran
to catch	caught	to see	saw
to cut	cut	to sell	sold
to do	did	to sit	sat
to find	found	to speak	spoke
to fly	flew	to stand	stood
to go	went	to take	took
to have	had	to teach	taught
to hit	hit	to throw	threw
to lose	lost	to write	wrote

You will find a complete list of irregular tense formations in the appendix.

Use the past tense of *to be* (*was/were*) plus an *-ing* ending on the verb to form the past tense of an action in progress or incomplete. There is no difference for regular or irregular verbs:

> to sing → was singing
> to go → was going
> to carry → was carrying, and so on

Use the past tense of *to do* (*did*) to form the past tense of an emphatic response.

Let's compare the three past tense formations:

Habitual Statement (something done frequently)
I spoke English.
We went to school.
They played soccer.

In Progress (incomplete)
I was speaking English.
We were going to school.
They were playing soccer.

Emphatic Response
"You did not speak English." → "I *did* speak English."
"We went to school." → "We *did not* go to school."
"They did not play soccer." → "They *did* play soccer."

Questions and negations with *not* are formed with the past tense of *to do* (*did*) in the same way they are formed in the present tense:

Present Tense	Past Tense
Does he like the article?	Did he like the article?
You do not understand.	You did not understand.

exercise	5-11

Rewrite each sentence in the past tense.

1. Susan helps her friends.

   _____

2. We go to the movies.

   _____

3. She is washing the car.

   _____

4. My father is in the kitchen.

   _____

5. She does not understand you.

   _____

6. Are you satisfied?

   _____

7. Do you always speak Spanish?

   _____

8. The girls are riding on a horse.

   _____

9. He catches the ball.

   _____

10. They play chess after supper.

    _____

11. Someone has my wallet.

    _____

12. Does Mr. Ibrahim live here?

    _____

13. They are learning a new language.

    _____

14. Karen works in New Orleans.

_____

15. You often make mistakes.

_____

exercise	5-12

Change the habitual past tense to a past tense action in progress or incomplete.

EXAMPLE: I studied it.
I was studying it.

1. He wrote a letter.

_____

2. My mother sat in the garden.

_____

3. Jim stood next to Alicia.

_____

4. The man brought us some fish.

_____

5. We lost the game.

_____

6. The boys hurried home.

_____

7. The dog buried a bone in the yard.

_____

8. I had a bad day.

_____

9. They went to the store.

_____

10. He stayed with an uncle.

_____

exercise   5-13

Change each past tense sentence to a question.

1. They made some mistakes.

_____

2. Will played a few games of cards.

_____

3. The girls saw the comet.

_____

4. Her aunt carried the basket into the kitchen.

_____

5. They were in the city all day.

_____

6. Garth learned a good lesson.

_____

7. She was home all day.

_____

8. Robert had the radio.

_____

9. The woman ran for the bus.

_____

10. The dogs fought over a bone.

_____

The Present Perfect Tense

To express something that began in the past and continues until the present use the present perfect tense. This tense has two formations: (1) the habitual or frequent action and (2) the action in progress or incomplete. The habitual present perfect tense is formed by conjugating *to have* (*have/has*) in the present tense and combining it with a past participle:

to work → has worked
to carry → has carried
to speak → has spoken

The participle of a regular verb looks just like the past tense. It ends in -ed. But the participle of an irregular verb often makes a change. Look at this list of irregular participles of commonly used verbs:

Infinitive	Participle	Infinitive	Participle
to be	been	to make	made
to break	broken	to put	put
to bring	brought	to read	read
to build	built	to ride	ridden
to buy	bought	to run	run
to catch	caught	to see	seen
to cut	cut	to sell	sold
to do	done	to sit	sat
to find	found	to speak	spoken
to fly	flown	to stand	stood
to go	gone	to take	taken
to have	had	to teach	taught
to hit	hit	to throw	thrown
to lose	lost	to write	written

The present perfect of an action in progress or incomplete is formed by conjugating *to have* (*have/has*) with the participle of *to be* (*been*) and the verb with an *-ing* ending. The structure is *to have + been +* **verb**-*ing*:

> to work → has been working
> to carry → has been carrying
> to speak → has been speaking

In this formation there is no need to worry about irregular participles.

Notice how the present perfect tense forms from the present tense:

He learns English.	He has learned English
He is learning English.	He has been learning English.
We see strangers.	We have seen strangers.
We are seeing strangers.	We have been seeing strangers.
I ride a long time.	I have ridden a long time.
I am riding a long time.	I have been riding a long time.

exercise   5-14

Change the habitual present perfect tense to the present perfect tense of an action in progress or incomplete.

1. Lana has spoken with him.

_____

2. Has he gone to his class?

_____

3. I have worked all day.

_____

4. The tourists have flown around the world.

_____

5. My parents have walked along the river.

_____

6. Has the boy put his toys away?

_____

7. She has taught us all that she knows.

_____

exercise   5-15

Rewrite the present tense sentences in the present perfect tense.

1. Ms. Nellum takes the boy home.

_____

2. We ride on a bus.

_____

3. They are riding their bikes.

_____

4. Do you often make cookies?

_____

5. She does not understand.

_____

6. They are doing their homework.

_____

7. I am going to the same class.

_____

8. He often breaks his bat.

_____

9. They are breaking windows.

_____

10. Juanita writes her a letter.

_____

exercise	5-16

Circle the boldface word that best completes each sentence.

1. Mike has **borrowed/borrowing** my dictionary.

2. We have **been/went** driving all day.

3. **Does/Has** she made fresh bread?

4. Marie **did/has** found your wallet.

5. I have been **listening/listened** to the radio.

6. They have **going/been** home all day.

7. My sister has **going/been** working in the city.

8. **She/They** have taken my money.

9. We have been **hurried/hurrying** to catch the bus.

10. Have you **wrote/written** the postcards?

The Past Perfect Tense

To express an action that began in the past and ended in the past use the past perfect tense. It has two formations similar to the present perfect tense. But in the past perfect tense, the verb _to have_ is conjugated in the past tense (_had_):

> to work → had worked/had been working
> to carry → had carried/had been carrying
> to speak → had spoken/had been speaking.

You can form a question in the present perfect or past perfect tenses by inverting the verb and the subject:

> You have spoken. → Have you spoken?
> He had learned. → Had he learned?

You can form the negative by placing _not_ after _have_ or _had_:

> You have spoken. → You have not spoken.
> He had learned. → He had not learned.

exercise   5-17

Rewrite the present perfect tense sentences in the past perfect tense.

1. Julio has written him a few letters.

   _____

2. I have been writing a novel.

   _____

3. Have you seen a doctor?

   _____

4. She has cut her finger.

   _____

5. The girls have stayed home again.

   _____

exercise   5-18

Rewrite the present tense sentences in the past perfect tense.

1. The woman takes the girl home.

   _____

2. We ride on a train.

   _____

3. I always speak Spanish.

   _____

4. Do you often make roast beef?

   _____

5. Rebecca does not remember.

   _____

6. Is he doing his best?

   _____

7. I am going to the movies.

   _____

8. Cindy teaches us English.

_____

9. We play the same game.

_____

10. Bethany writes in her diary.

_____

The Future Tense

The future tense can be expressed in a few ways. One of the most common is to use the present tense but to imply a future tense meaning. This is done by using the present tense verb formation for an action in progress or incomplete. Look at the following examples:

> Ray is going to school *today*. (present tense)
> Ray is going to school *tomorrow*. (future tense)

> They are traveling to Mexico *today*. (present tense)
> They are traveling to Mexico *tomorrow*. (future tense)

Another way to form the future tense is to combine the verb *shall* or *will* with an infinitive. If the action is one in progress or incomplete, use the structure *shall/will* + *be* + **verb**-*ing*:

> to go → I shall go/I shall be going
> to speak → he will speak/he will be speaking

Let's look at the complete conjugation:

Pronoun	Habitual Action	Incomplete Action
I	shall speak	shall be speaking
you	will try	will be trying
he, she, it	will make	will be making
we	shall read	shall be reading
they	will work	will be working

Traditionally, *shall* has been used for the first-person singular and plural (*I* and *we*). However, many modern speakers of English use only *will*.

Form a question in the future by inverting the verb and the subject:

> You will sing. → Will you sing?

Form the negative by placing *not* after *will*:

> You will sing. → You will not sing.

exercise	5-19

Rewrite the following present tense sentences in the future tense by using will.

1. The girls play soccer.

   _____

2. I am learning to drive.

   _____

3. We are not home on time.

   _____

4. Do you recognize him?

   _____

5. Trent is driving to Texas.

   _____

6. The men work many hours.

   _____

7. She flies to London every year.

   _____

8. Dr. Saloff does not treat her asthma.

   _____

9. The little boy loses his place.

   _____

10. Is he going to the university?

   _____

The Future Perfect Tense

The future perfect tense describes an action that begins and ends in the future tense. Just like other perfect tenses, it has two formations: one for a habitual or frequent action and one for an action in progress or incomplete. The structure for a habitual action is *will* + *have* + **past participle**:

> to work → will have worked
> to see → will have seen

The structure for an action in progress or incomplete is *will* + *have* + *been* + **verb**-*ing*:

> to work → will have been working
> to see → will have been seeing

Let's look at the complete conjugation:

Pronoun	Habitual Action	Incomplete Action
I	will have spoken	will have been speaking
you	will have tried	will have been trying
he, she, it	will have made	will have been making
we	will have read	will have been reading
they	will have worked	will have been working

exercise   5-20

Rewrite the present tense sentences in the future perfect tense.

1. My father takes the girl to school.

   _____

2. We ride on the subway.

   _____

3. They are riding their bikes.

   _____

4. Do you make candy?

   _____

5. She does not understand.

   _____

6. Do they do the work?

   _____

7. I am going to the same class.

   _____

8. Chet breaks his finger.

   _____

9. She arrives by ten.

   _____

10. Sabrina writes several notes.

    _____

Comparison of Regular and Irregular Verbs

The regular verbs are the easiest to work with. Since there are no unusual changes to make in the conjugations, they follow very neat patterns. With irregular verbs, you must remember that the past tense and the participle are formed with vowel changes. Let's look at three verbs and how they appear in all the tenses:

Tense	to play	to go	to sing
Present	he plays	he goes	he sings
	he is playing	he is going	he is singing
	he does play	he does go	he does sing
Past	he played	he went	he sang
	he was playing	he was going	he was singing
	he did play	he did go	he did sing
Present Perfect	he has played	he has gone	he has sung
	he has been playing	he has been going	he has been singing
Past Perfect	he had played	he had gone	he had sung
	he had been playing	he had been going	he had been singing
Future	he will play	he will go	he will sing
	he will be playing	he will be going	he will be singing
Future Perfect	he will have played	he will have gone	he will have sung
	he will have been playing	he will have been going	he will have been singing

exercise **5-21**

Rewrite the following present tense sentences in the other five tenses.

1. Sig buys a car.

   past _____

   present perfect _____

   past perfect _____

   future _____

   future perfect _____

2. I am helping them.

   past _____

   present perfect _____

   past perfect _____

   future _____

   future perfect _____

3. We come home late.

past _____

present perfect _____

past perfect _____

future _____

future perfect _____

Going to and *used to* are two important phrases that cause a tense change. Use *going to* as a substitute for *shall* or *will* in the future tense. Use *used to* as a substitute for the simple past tense. Combine *going to* or *used to* with an infinitive:

> He will learn English. → He is going to learn English.
> He spoke English. → He used to speak English.

When you use *to be going to* to express the future tense, you imply that the action is something you *intend* to do. When you use *used to* to express the past tense, you imply that the action is something that had been *a habit.*

You can also use *going to* in the past tense (*was/were going to*) to express something that you *had intended* doing:

> I was going to buy a new car but changed my mind.
> Were you going to visit your aunt?

exercise	5-22

Rewrite the following present tense sentences (1) in the future tense with going to *and (2) in the past tense with* used to.

1. Bill takes a class at the university.

   _____

   _____

2. We travel to Germany.

   _____

   _____

3. I have lots of parties.

   _____

   _____

4. Do you live in Ecuador?

   _____

   _____

5. The children watch television every evening.

_____

_____

6. Does she spend a lot of money?

_____

_____

Rewrite the following past tense sentences with to be going to *in the past tense.*

    EXAMPLE: I read the novel.
        I was going to read the novel.

7. They sold the old SUV.

_____

8. Liz began her studies at the university.

_____

9. The twins lived together in San Francisco.

_____

10. Did the attorney find a new witness?

_____

Auxiliary Verbs

You have already encountered three **auxiliary** (or **helping**) verbs: *be*, *do*, and *have*. They are conjugated and used with another verb to change that verb's meaning or tense:

> I go → I *am* going (changed to in progress or incomplete)

> you sing → *do* you sing? (changed to a question)

> she makes → she *has* made (changed to the present perfect tense)

There are several other auxiliary verbs you should know. Note that many of the auxiliary verbs cannot be used in all tenses. And in some cases, you have to change to a different verb to form a specific tense. The following examples will be conjugated with the third-person pronoun *he*:

	to be able to	**to be supposed to**
Present	is able to	is supposed to
Past	was able to	was supposed to
Present Perfect	has been able to	has been supposed to
Past Perfect	had been able to	had been supposed to
Future	will be able to	will be supposed to
Future Perfect	will have been able to	will have been supposed to

	can	**to have to**
Present	can	has to
Past	could **OR** was able to	had to
Present Perfect	has been able to	has had to
Past Perfect	had been able to	had had to
Future	will be able to	will have to
Future Perfect	will have been able to	will have had to

	may	must
Present	may	must
Past	might	had to
Present Perfect	N/A	has had to
Past Perfect	N/A	had had to
Future	N/A	will have to
Future Perfect	N/A	will have had to

	ought to	should
Present	ought to	should
Past	N/A	N/A
Present Perfect	N/A	N/A
Past Perfect	N/A	N/A
Future	N/A	N/A
Future Perfect	N/A	N/A

	to want to	to need to
Present	wants	needs to
Past	wanted	needed to
Present Perfect	has wanted	has needed to
Past Perfect	had wanted	had needed to
Future	will want	will need to
Future Perfect	will have wanted	will have needed to

Auxiliary verbs like these are followed by an infinitive:

I can *go*.	I want to *go*.
You must *learn*.	You have to *learn*.
We should *help*.	We need to *help*.
He can *drive*.	He ought to *drive*.

exercise   6-1

Rewrite each sentence twice in the present tense: once by adding can *and once by adding* want to.

1. Serena buys a new car.

   _____

   _____

2. We borrow some money.

   _____

   _____

3. I leave at ten o'clock.

   _____

   _____

4. The boys have cereal for breakfast.

   _____

   _____

5. My sister is home by 6:00 P.M.

   _____

   _____

6. They travel to California.

   _____

   _____

7. Mr. Gutierrez carries the groceries for her.

   _____

   _____

exercise   6-2

Remove the auxiliary in each sentence and rewrite the sentence appropriately.

1. You ought to stay in bed all day.

   _____

2. I should try hard.

   _____

3. My brother may be a little late.

   _____

4. We need to find a room for the night.

   _____

5. Ms. Brown is able to get out of bed today.

   _____

6. Ramon must remain at home today.

   _____

7. They have to learn to behave well.

   _____

8. Can you hear me?

_____

9. His girlfriend wants to sell her condo.

_____

10. Do you have to work every day?

_____

When you use some of the auxiliaries with a verb, you tell to what degree of obligation someone has to carry out the action of the verb. Look at the sentences below. The first one shows the least degree of obligation. This is something someone doesn't have to do. The last sentence shows the greatest degree of obligation. This is something that someone absolutely must do.

"We may return the books." (Least obligation. It's our choice.)
"We can return the books." (Little obligation. It's our choice.)
"We are able to return the books." (Little obligation. We have the ability to do this.)
"We need to return the books." (Slight obligation.)
"We ought to return the books." (Little obligation, but this would be a good idea.)
"We should return the books." (Little obligation, but this would be a good idea.)
"We are supposed to return the books." (Some obligation. Someone has suggested we do this.)
"We must return the books." (Greatest obligation. It is our duty to do this.)
"We have to return the books." (Greatest obligation. It is our duty to do this.)

When you add an auxiliary to a sentence, use the same tense for the auxiliary as that of the original verb. For example: "Celeste found (past tense) a recent biography." When you add _have to_ to that sentence, you say, "Celeste had to (past tense) find a recent biography."

exercise | **6-3**

Rewrite the following sentences with the auxiliary shown in parentheses. Be sure to keep the same tense as in the original sentence.

1. Mr. Weston drives to Arizona. (to have to)

_____

2. We borrowed some tools from him. (to need to)

_____

3. I left for Mexico on the tenth of May. (to want to)

_____

4. Ms. McAdam will help you. (to be able to)

_____

5. Jolene repairs the car. (ought to)

   _____

6. Did you understand them? (can)

   _____

7. Aaron worked on Saturday. (to be supposed to)

   _____

8. She orders the cake today. (must)

   _____

9. Have you filled out the application? (to be able to)

   _____

10. Our neighbors will paint their house. (to want to)

   _____

Unit 7

Passive Voice

The **passive voice** is a structure that allows you to make a statement without knowing who performed the action of the sentence: *The house was destroyed.* Or the person who performed the action is placed in a *passive position* in the sentence: *The house was destroyed by soldiers.*

An *active* sentence is commonly structured *subject + verb + direct object*. A *passive* sentence changes that structure to *direct object* used as the *subject + to be + past participle + by + subject* used as the *object of the preposition*. Let's compare the two structures:

Active Sentences	Passive Sentences
Kim finds the dog.	The dog is found by Kim.
We buy his car.	His car is bought by us.
The girls stole the purse.	The purse was stolen by the girls.
They solved the problem.	The problem was solved by them.

The verb *to be* in the passive sentences is conjugated in the same tense as the verb in the active sentences. Look how the various tenses appear in the passive:

Tense	Passive Sentences
Present	The house is destroyed by the soldiers.
Past	The house was destroyed by the soldiers.
Present Perfect	The house has been destroyed by the soldiers.
Past Perfect	The house had been destroyed by the soldiers.
Future	The house will be destroyed by the soldiers.
Future Perfect	The house will have been destroyed by the soldiers.

Only in the present and past tenses is there a difference between the habitual form of the conjugation and the conjugation for an action in progress or incomplete:

the house is destroyed/the house is being destroyed
the house was destroyed/the house was being destroyed

exercise   7-1

Rewrite the passive sentences below as an action in progress. Keep the same tense.

1. Glenda is kissed by Stuart.

   _____

2. She was spoiled by her parents.

   _____

3. My eyes are tested in the clinic.

   _____

4. They were arrested for a crime.

   _____

5. Monique is awarded a medal.

   _____

6. The treasure was buried on an island.

   _____

7. The dog is punished again.

   _____

8. Was the old barn burned down?

   _____

exercise   7-2

Rewrite the passive sentences below in the present perfect tense.

1. We were punished by Father.

   _____

2. The men are taken prisoner.

   _____

3. She is thanked by the happy tourists.

   _____

4. I was beaten by a robber.

   _____

5. The car was not washed again.

   _____

6. Tony is examined by the doctor.

   _____

7. They are surrounded by the enemy.

   _____

8. Was your sister fired from her job?

   _____

9. Was the baby carried to his bedroom?

   _____

10. She is congratulated by her boss.

   _____

exercise | **7-3**

Rewrite the following active sentences as passive sentences. Keep the same tense.

1. A storm destroyed the cottage.

   _____

2. Did Columbus discover the New World?

   _____

3. They will buy our house.

   _____

4. My grandmother has baked the cakes.

   _____

5. Phil is cutting the bread.

   _____

6. Sergio was selling the newspapers.

   _____

7. Has Iris taken the money?

_____

8. She will kiss the baby.

_____

9. Is Max building the fence?

_____

10. Her brother forgot the map.

_____

Subjunctive Mood

The **subjunctive** is used in some limited but important ways. It is used to express a demand, suggestion, or request (*I suggest you **be** on time.*); to express a wish (*If only Jim **were** here.*); or to set a condition for a future action (*We **would leave** if the storm **would let up**.*). To understand these uses, you need to examine the subjunctive conjugations.

The present tense subjunctive is formed from the infinitive of a verb minus the particle word *to*. Notice that each pronoun requires the identical verb form:

Pronoun	to be	to go	to have	to work
I	be	go	have	work
you	be	go	have	work
he, she, it	be	go	have	work
we	be	go	have	work
they	be	go	have	work

The past tense subjunctive is formed from the plural past tense of either a regular or an irregular verb. Notice again that each pronoun requires the identical verb form:

Pronoun	to be	to go	to have	to work
I	were	went	had	worked
you	were	went	had	worked
he, she, it	were	went	had	worked
we	were	went	had	worked
they	were	went	had	worked

A third subjunctive conjugation is formed with the word *would* together with an infinitive, or *would have* plus a *past participle*. Look at these examples:

Indicative Sentences	Subjunctive Sentences
He is here.	He would be here.
She buys a book.	She would buy a book.
We have spoken.	We would have spoken.
I have played.	I would have played.

The present tense subjunctive is used to express a demand, suggestion, or request. In these instances, the subjunctive must be used in place of a regular present tense conjugation. Notice that it is optional to use the conjunction *that*. Consider these sentences:

> She demanded you *be* on time tomorrow. (not *are*)
> She demanded **that** you *be* on time tomorrow.
>
> I suggested he *come* by for a visit. (not *comes*)
> I suggested **that** he *come* by for a visit.
>
> The judge requested the lawyer *have* the documents prepared. (not *has*)
> The judge requested **that** the lawyer *have* the documents prepared.

This same structure is used with a few other similar verbs: *to command, to order, to propose.*

The past tense subjunctive is often used to express a wish:

> I wish Ahmed *were* my brother.
> She wished she *had* enough money for a car.
> If only my mother *worked* for him, too.
> The children wish it already *were* Christmas.

Note that a wish can be expressed by beginning a sentence with *if* or *if only.*

You should be aware that *were* is sometimes avoided in casual conversation and is frequently replaced by the simple past tense verb *was* with singular subjects (e.g., *I wish Ahmed* **was** *my brother.*).

The subjunctive formed with *would* is used when there are two clauses in a sentence and one of them is an *if*-clause. This kind of sentence sets a condition in one clause for the action to occur in the second clause. The past tense subjunctive is used in the *if*-clause. The word *would* appears in the clause that does *not* begin with *if*. Some examples:

> If Nadia *were* here, Mother *would be* very happy.
> If I *had* a million dollars, I *would buy* a big house.
> She *would travel* to Spain if her uncle *invited* her.
> Mr. Perez *would learn* English if he *lived* in Texas.

These sentences mean that the action would happen in the present or the future if the conditions were right.

> **This would happen if these conditions were right.**
> She *would travel* to Spain if her uncle *invited* her.

The same format is required even if the verbs are structured like the present perfect tense (*I have gone, you have seen,* etc.):

> If Nadia *had been* here, Mother *would have been* very happy.
> Mr. Perez *would have learned* English if he *had lived* in Texas.

These sentences mean that the action would have happened in the past if the conditions had been right.

> **This would have happened if these conditions had been right.**
> Mr. Perez *would have learned* English if he *had lived* in Texas.

exercise   8-1

Combine the phrase in parentheses with the indicative sentence. Change the verb to the present tense subjunctive.

EXAMPLE: (I demand . . .) He gives me the money.
I demand he give me the money.

1. (She demands . . .) Forrest returns home by 5:00 P.M.

_____

2. (The man suggests . . .) You wear a shirt and tie to work.

_____

3. (They requested . . .) I am a little more helpful.

_____

4. (My father demanded . . .) We pay for the damage to the car.

_____

5. (Did he suggest . . . ?) She comes in for an interview.

_____

6. (Roger demands that . . .) The boy has enough to eat.

_____

7. (Did Mother request that . . . ?) Her will is read aloud.

_____

8. (He has suggested that . . .) We are trained for other jobs.

_____

9. (Who demanded that . . .?) The statue is erected on this site.

_____

10. (Did he suggest . . . ?) The mayor finds a new assistant.

_____

exercise   8-2

Complete each phrase below with any appropriate sentence.

1. He demands _____.

2. We suggest _____.

3. Dwayne requests _____.

4. I must demand that _____.

5. Will you suggest to him that _____?

exercise   8-3

Rewrite the following sentences in the past tense subjunctive. Begin each one with the phrase I wish.

1. Becca is here today.

   _____

2. We are having a big party for Grandmother.

   _____

3. He has enough money to buy a condo.

   _____

4. My friends have come for a visit.

   _____

5. Darnell doesn't need an operation.

   _____

6. His uncle drives slowly.

   _____

7. I can borrow some money from you.

   _____

8. The weather is not so rainy.

   _____

9. They help me every day.

   _____

10. She wants to go on vacation with me.

    _____

exercise 8-4

Combine the following phrases with the sentence shown in parentheses.

 EXAMPLE: If you were here, . . . (I am happy.)
 If you were here, I would be happy.

1. If Evelyn were older, . . . (Garrett asks her out.)

 _____

2. If I had more time, . . . (I go to the store.)

 _____

3. If you spoke louder, . . . (He hears you.)

 _____

4. If it were colder, . . . (I turn on the heat.)

 _____

5. If my brother came along, . . . (He helps me wash the car.)

 _____

6. She would make a cake if . . . (It is Erin's birthday.)

 _____

7. Gary would rent an apartment here if . . . (He likes the neighborhood.)

 _____

8. The boys would play soccer if . . . (Someone has a soccer ball.)

 _____

9. I would speak Spanish if . . . (I live in Puerto Rico.)

 _____

10. The doctor would come to our house if . . . (The baby is sick.)

 _____

exercise   8-5

Rewrite the following sentences using the present perfect tense for the verbs.

      EXAMPLE: He would buy a car if he had the money.
              He would have bought a car if he had had the money.

1. She would sell me her bicycle if she bought a new one.

    _____

2. If you came early you would meet my cousin.

    _____

3. If only Karen were here.

    _____

4. The children would play in the yard if it were not raining.

    _____

5. If the lawyer found the document he would win his case.

    _____

6. If only my mother were able to walk again.

    _____

7. Juanita would travel to New York if she got the job.

    _____

8. If he found the wallet he would give it to Rick.

    _____

9. Jackie would want to come along if he had more time.

    _____

10. If only they understood the problem.

    _____

Adverbs

You already know that adjectives modify nouns. For example: the *blue* house, our *little* brother, a *silly* poem. **Adverbs** are also modifiers, but they modify verbs, adjectives, and other adverbs. You can easily identify adverbs because most end in *-ly*: *happily, quickly, slowly, beautifully.*

Most adjectives can be changed to an adverb by adding *-ly* to the end of the adjective. If the adjective ends in *-y*, change the *-y* to *-i* and then add *-ly*.

Adjective	Adverb
bad	badly
bright	brightly
cold	coldly
happy	happily
merry	merrily
speedy	speedily
sudden	suddenly
wrong	wrongly

There are a few adjectives and adverbs that have special forms and uses. One important one is *good*. If *good* means "kind," it is only used as an adjective. Use *kindly* in place of it as an adverb. If *good* means "talented," use *well* as its adverb. Careful! If *well* means "healthy," it is not an adverb; it is an adjective.

good = kind: He is a *good* man.
               He spoke to us *kindly.*

good = talented: Hayley is a *good* tennis player.
                   Hayley plays tennis *well.*

well = healthy: I am glad that your father is *well* again.

There is only one form for the word *fast.* It is both an adjective and an adverb:

Lee is a *fast* talker. (adjective)
Lee talks *fast.* (adverb)

And note that the adverb *home* does not end in *-ly*:

> We went *home* after work.

You can also identify adverbs by asking certain questions of the verb in a sentence. Ask *how, where,* or *when.* The answer is an adverb.

How? Where? When?	The Answer = Adverb
Jamal got quickly to his feet.	
"How did Jamal get to his feet?"	quickly
She went home on the bus.	
"Where did she go on the bus?"	home
They arrived punctually.	
"When did they arrive?"	punctually

Some adverbs of time, which answer the question *when,* do not always end in *-ly.* Consider these words: *today, tomorrow, yesterday, tonight, late, early, never.*

Certain adverbs, which often do not end in *-ly,* qualify *the degree* of the meaning of an adjective or adverb: *quite, rather, very, somewhat, too:*

> somewhat slowly = the slowness is not great but evident
> rather slowly = the slowness is emphasized, but it is not extreme
> quite slowly = the slowness is emphasized here
> very slowly = the slowness is extreme
> too slowly = the slowness is more than desired

Let's look at how adverbs can modify verbs, adjectives, and other adverbs:

Verbs	Adjectives	Adverbs
Justin walked *slowly.*	It is an *extremely* strange idea.	She ran *very* fast.
The boys drove *home.*	I have a *very* bad cold.	He sang *too* quietly.
Hannah laughed *loudly.*	It was a *rather* stupid question.	I sighed *rather* sadly.
Carmen writes *carelessly.*	He was *partially* dressed.	He smiled *quite* cheerfully.

exercise	9-1

Change the adjective in parentheses to an adverb. Place it appropriately in the sentence.

1. My sister walked into the room. (timid)

   _____

2. We sat down next to the bed. (quiet)

   _____

3. Harvey spoke angrily to the man. (rather)

   _____

4. The children entered the classroom. (noisy)

   _____

5. He said that my story was boring. (too)

   _____

6. She talked to the little girl. (harsh)

   _____

7. Julia followed the pretty girl. (home)

   _____

8. My uncle is a smart man. (very)

   _____

9. My cousin plays the piano. (good)

   _____

10. The animal stared into my face. (cold)

   _____

exercise   9-2

Using the adverbial phrases in parentheses, write appropriate sentences.

1. (very neatly) _____

2. (well) _____

3. (sadly) _____

4. (too) _____

5. (rather quickly) _____

6. (yesterday) _____

7. (never) _____

8. (quite strongly) _____

9. (too carelessly) _____

10. (so beautifully) _____

Contractions

Contractions are a combination of two words. Often they are a pronoun and a verb. But not all verbs can be combined with a pronoun to form a contraction. Use only these verbs: *have, has, is, are, am, would,* and *will.* Look how these verbs form contractions with the pronouns:

Pronoun	have/has	is/are/am	would/will
I	I've	I'm	I'd/I'll
you	you've	you're	you'd/you'll
he	he's	he's	he'd/he'll
she	she's	she's	she'd/she'll
it	it's	it's	N/A
we	we've	we're	we'd/we'll
they	they've	they're	they'd/they'll
who	who's	who's	who'd/who'll

Certain verbs form contractions with the negative word *not*:

Verb	Contraction
are	aren't
can	can't
could	couldn't
did	didn't
do	don't
does	doesn't
has	hasn't
have	haven't
is	isn't
must	mustn't
need	needn't
should	shouldn't
was	wasn't
were	weren't
will	won't
would	wouldn't

exercise   10-1

Rewrite the pronoun and verb in each sentence as a contraction.

1. You have been very unhappy. _____

2. I am not going to work today. _____

3. He would enjoy this movie a lot. _____

4. They are my best friends. _____

5. It is very cold today. _____

6. She will stop by for a visit tomorrow. _____

7. Who has been using my computer? _____

8. He is a very fine teacher. _____

9. We have never seen anything like this. _____

10. I will join you for dinner tomorrow. _____

11. She is a great soccer player. _____

12. Who would want to live in this neighborhood? _____

13. You are spending too much money. _____

14. They have gone to the United States. _____

15. It has been a very humid day. _____

exercise   10-2

Rewrite the verb and not *in each sentence as a contraction.*

1. You must not act surprised. _____

2. He cannot go to school today. _____

3. Mother will not allow that to happen. _____

4. The boys could not know what danger there was. _____

5. They are not acting properly. _____

6. Did you not do the housework? _____

7. My cousin was not at work today. _____

8. The girls do not like Mark. _____

9. Is that man not your uncle? _____

10. We should not spend so much time together. _____

| exercise | 10-3 |

Write original sentences with the contractions given in parentheses.

1. (hasn't) _____

2. (mustn't) _____

3. (shouldn't) _____

4. (needn't) _____

5. (weren't) _____

6. (I've) _____

7. (he'll) _____

8. (they're) _____

9. (you'd) _____

10. (she's) _____

Plurals

Most English **plurals** are formed quite simply. Just add *-s* to the end of a noun:

> dog → dogs
> building → buildings

However, if the noun ends in *-s, -ss, -z, -x, -ch,* or *-sh,* add *-es* to form the plural:

> boss → bosses
> box → boxes
> witch → witches
> dish → dishes

If the noun ends in a consonant plus *-y,* change the *-y* to *-i,* then add *-es*:

> lady → ladies
> penny → pennies

Words that end in *-o* are a special problem. Some form their plural by adding *-s,* and others form their plural by adding *-es.* Look at these examples:

Singular	Plural + *-s*	Singular	Plural + *-es*
auto	autos	potato	potatoes
piano	pianos	hero	heroes
alto	altos	echo	echoes
zoo	zoos	veto	vetoes
solo	solos	cargo	cargoes

Consult a dictionary to know precisely which plural ending to use with words that end in *-o.*

There are a few words that form the plural with an -s ending but also require a consonant change in which *f* changes to *v*:

knife → knives
leaf → leaves
shelf → shelves
wife → wives
wolf → wolves

Certain other nouns form their plural in completely irregular ways. Fortunately, the list is quite brief:

child → children
mouse → mice
foot → feet
person → people (or persons)
goose → geese
deer → deer [no change!]
man → men
woman → women
tooth → teeth
ox → oxen

exercise   11-1

Write the plural form of the following words.

1. house _____

2. wife _____

3. ox _____

4. fox _____

5. tooth _____

6. mouse _____

7. fez _____

8. person _____

9. candy _____

10. veto _____

11. deer _____

12. factory _____

13. leaf _____

14. university _____

15. jury _____

exercise   11-2

Change each noun in the following sentences to the plural. Make any necessary changes to the verbs.

1. The boy is chasing the little mouse.

_____

2. His brother is putting the pot in the box.

   _____

3. Does the teacher know the man?

   _____

4. The hero of the story was a child.

   _____

5. My friend wants to buy the knife, spoon, and dish.

   _____

6. A goose is flying over the field.

   _____

7. The clumsy person hurt my foot.

   _____

8. The poor woman has a broken tooth.

   _____

9. We saw a wild ox in the zoo.

   _____

10. The ugly witch wanted the trained wolf.

    _____

Punctuation

The **period** is a commonly used signal that a sentence has ended. It is used after two types of sentences: (1) *the declarative sentence*, which is a statement about something, and (2) *the imperative sentence*, which is a request or command:

Statement: I have five dollars in my pocket.

Command: Give me the five dollars that you have in your pocket.

The period is also used after an abbreviation. Some abbreviations are titles: *Mr., Mrs., Ms., Dr., Rev.* Others are short versions of specific expressions: *A.M., P.M.,* etc. If you end a sentence with one of these abbreviations, *do not add a second period.* For example:

Phillip arrived at exactly 8:00 P.M.

The **question mark** at the end of a sentence signals that the sentence is asking a question. You already know how to position verbs to form a question. Some examples:

Statement	Question
Carlotta is at home.	Is Carlotta at home?
You have a problem.	Do you have a problem?
They were in Rome.	Were they in Rome?

The **exclamation point** at the end of a sentence signals that the information in the sentence is stated strongly or with emotion. Some ordinary statements and exclamations look identical. But if the sentence ends in an exclamation point, it is expressed with emotion:

Ordinary Statement	Strong Statement
Jason is sick.	Jason is sick!
I saw a stranger there.	I saw a stranger there!
It has started to snow.	It has started to snow!
He didn't leave.	He didn't leave!

exercise 12-1

Place either a period, an exclamation point, or a question mark at the end of each sentence.

1. She took a book from the shelf and began to read_____

2. Do you like living in California_____

3. She asked me if I know her brother_____

4. Sit down and make yourself comfortable_____

5. Shut up_____

6. How many years were you in the army_____

7. I can't believe it's storming again_____

8. When did they arrive_____

9. Watch out_____

10. Her little brother is about eight years old_____

The **comma** is the signal in the middle of a sentence that ideas are being separated. This can be done to avoid confusing the ideas or to separate things in a list. For example, compare the sentence "When he came in the house was cold." to "When he came in, the house was cold." You do not mean that "he came in the house." There are two ideas here in two clauses. They are separated by a comma: (1) He came in. (2) The house was cold.

As an example of a list, consider the sentence "He bought pop, tarts, and candy." If you omit the comma after *pop*, someone might think that he bought *pop tarts*.

In a list, there should be a comma after every item until you use the word *and: a boy, a girl, two dogs,* and *a cat.* Some English writers prefer to omit the comma before *and*.

> I need paint, brushes, a yardstick, and some tape.

> **OR**

> I need paint, brushes, a yardstick and some tape.

Commas are also used to separate the name of a person to whom an imperative or a question is directed:

> Janelle, call Mr. Montoya on the telephone.
> Dr. Gillespie, will my husband be all right?
> Boys, try to be a little quieter.

They are also often needed to separate two or more adjectives that modify a noun:

> She wore a red, woolen jacket.
> The tall, muscular man was a weightlifter.

You should use a comma to separate two independent clauses combined as a compound sentence. They are most often combined with these conjunctions: *and, but, for, not, or, so,* and *yet.* An independent clause is one that has a subject and predicate and makes sense when it stands alone. Some examples:

> DeWitt is baking a cake, and Allison is preparing the roast.
> Do you want to go to a movie, or should we just stay home?
> It began to rain hard, yet they continued on the hike.

You should separate exclamations and common expressions from the rest of the sentence with a comma:

> Oh, I can't believe you said that!
> No, I don't live in Germany anymore.
> Yes, you can go outside now.
> Well, you really look beautiful tonight.
> By the way, my mother is coming for a visit.

A comma is required to separate the day of the week from the date, and the day of the month from the year. The comma is omitted if only the month and year are given.

> He arrived here on Monday, June 1st.
> My birthday is January 8, 1989.
> The war ended in May 1945.

A **decimal point** looks like a period. In some languages, a decimal amount is separated by a comma: 6,25 or 95,75. But in American English, a decimal amount is separated by a period (a decimal point): 6.25 or 95.75.

In long numbers, amounts of thousands are separated by a comma in English. In other languages, they are often separated by a decimal point or by leaving a space:

English Numbers	Numbers in Other Languages
1,550,600	1.550.600 or 1 550 600
22,000,000	22.000.000 or 22 000 000

Rewrite each sentence and place commas where they are needed.

1. Ms. Muti please have a seat in my office.

_____

2. She bought chicken ham bread and butter.

_____

3. By the way your mother called about an hour ago.

_____

4. Paul was born on May 2 1989 and Caroline was born on June 5 1989.

   _____

5. No you may not go to the movies with Rich!

   _____

6. Well that was an interesting discussion.

   _____

7. The men sat on one side and the women sat on the other.

   _____

8. Oh the dress hat and gloves look beautiful on you Jane.

   _____

9. It happened on April 5 1999.

   _____

10. Yes I have a suitcase and flight bag with me.

   _____

The **colon** signals that a list of things or special related information follows. For example:

> You'll need certain tools for this project: a hammer, screwdriver, hacksaw, and chisel.
> I suddenly understood the plot of the story: A man steals a thousand dollars to help his dying son.

It is also used to separate the hour from the minutes when telling time: 5:30, 6:25 A.M., 11:45 P.M.

The **semicolon** is a punctuation mark that is similar to both a comma and a period. It signals that there is a pause between ideas, and those ideas are closely linked. It often combines two related independent clauses into one sentence:

> Jamal is a powerful runner; he is determined to win the race today.
> Loud music filled the room; everyone was dancing as if entranced.

exercise   12-3

In the blank, place either a colon or a semicolon.

1. There are some things you need for this recipe_____ sugar, salt, and flour.

2. She understood the meaning of the story_____ Thou shalt not kill.

3. Peter is an excellent swimmer_____ he coaches a team at our pool.

4. This document is important_____ it will prove his innocence.

5. Add these names to the list_____ Irena, Helen, Jaime, and Grace.

Quotation marks enclose the words that are said by someone. They indicate a direct quote. Look at the difference between a direct and indirect quote:

Direct Quote	Indirect Quote
He said, "Stay where you are."	He said that I should stay where I am.
She asked, "Is that Tran's brother?"	She asked if that is Tran's brother.

Remember that all punctuation marks that belong to the quoted sentence are enclosed *inside* the quotation marks:

> **Correct:** He asked, "Does she often visit you?"
> **Incorrect:** He asked, "Does she often visit you"?

The title of a short story or magazine article should be enclosed by quotation marks: *I just read "My Life on a Farm" by James Smith.* If a quote is located within a quote, it should be enclosed by *single* quotation marks: *He said, "I just read 'My Life on a Farm' by James Smith."*

exercise 12-4

Rewrite each sentence and add quotation marks where they are needed.

1. She asked, Why do you spend so much money?

   _____

2. I learned that from Tips for Dining Out in a restaurant magazine.

   _____

3. Rafael said, Elena's grandfather is very ill.

   _____

4. This is going to be a big problem, he said sadly.

   _____

5. Kurt will say, I already read The Ransom of Red Chief in school.

   _____

You already know that the **apostrophe** is used in forming contractions:

> I am → I'm
> we are → we're

The apostrophe is also used to form possessives. To make the meaning of a singular noun possessive, add -'s. For plural nouns that end in an -s, just add the apostrophe. All other plurals will end in -'s.

Noun	Possessive Form	Meaning
boy	the boy's dog	the dog that belongs to the boy
boys	the boys' games	the games that belong to the boys
house	the house's roof	the roof of the house
Tom	Tom's aunt	an aunt of Tom's
book	a book's pages	the pages of a book
men	the men's work	the work that the men do

If a word ends in an -s, you can add -'s to form the possessive when the pronunciation of the word requires another syllable in the possessive:

> Lois → Lois's
> Thomas → Thomas's
> actress → actress's

If another syllable is not pronounced to form the possessive, just add an apostrophe; this tends to be the case in the plural:

> actresses → actresses'
> railings → railings'
> classes → classes'

It is common to use an apostrophe to form the plural of abbreviations: *two Dr.'s, three M.D.'s, four Ph.D.'s.* The same is true when forming the plural of a number or letter: "You had better mind your *p*'s and *q*'s."

---

exercise　12-5

Rewrite each sentence and add apostrophes where they are needed.

1. The geeses eggs are well hidden.

   _____

2. She cant understand you.

   _____

3. Is Mr. Hancocks daughter still in college?

   _____

4. The two girls performance was very bad.

   _____

5. Ms. Yonans aunt still lives in Mexico.

   _____

6. She met several M.D.s at the party.

   _____

7. Do you know Mr. Richards?

   _____

8. The womens purses were all stolen.

   _____

9. He wont join the other Ph.D.s in their discussion.

   _____

10. It isnt right to take another mans possessions.

    _____

exercise   12-6

In the blank write in the missing form of punctuation.

1. Blake _____ will you please try to understand my problem?

2. They went to England _____ Wales, and Scotland.

3. Someone stole my money _____

4. She asked, _____ When is the train supposed to arrive?"

5. Mr. Wilson _____ s son wants to buy a house in Wisconsin.

6. I have the following documents _____ a will, a passport, and a visa.

7. Grandmother died September 11 _____ 1999.

8. Jack is a pilot _____ he flies around the world.

9. Well _____ I can't believe you came home on time.

10. Are you planning another vacation _____

Infinitives and Gerunds

You have already discovered **infinitives** and how they are used as verbs. But infinitives can be used in other ways as well.

They can be used as nouns: *To run would be cowardly.* (subject of the sentence)

They can be used as adverbs: *We came here to thank you.* (why we came)

They can be used as adjectives: *He is the man to trust.* (modifies *man*)

Gerunds look like present participles: a verb plus an *-ing* ending (*running, looking, buying,* etc.). But gerunds are different from present participles. Present participles are used to form an action in progress or incomplete: *I was running, she is speaking, they are helping.* And as a participle they can be used as adjectives. But a gerund is used as a noun. Look at these examples:

Present Participle	Gerund
She was baking cookies.	Baking takes a lot of time.
I am living alone.	I don't like living alone.
We have been relaxing at home.	Relaxing will help relieve the tension.
He was spelling the new words.	Spelling is my best subject.

exercise 13-1

Look at each sentence and decide how the infinitive is used. Then write noun, adverb, *or* adjective *in the blank provided.*

1. _____ I bought the car *to make* you happy.

2. _____ He doesn't like *to run* after a big dinner.

3. _____ The book *to read* is *Moby Dick.*

4. _____ She gave me a gift *to show* her gratitude.

5. _____ *To pay* taxes is a privilege.

exercise   13-2

Look at each sentence and decide how the italicized word is used. Then write verb, adjective, *or* noun *in the blank provided.*

1. _____ *Running* water is a modern convenience.

2. _____ We are *taking* the family on a picnic.

3. _____ This is a *continuing* problem.

4. _____ *Playing* in the street is dangerous.

5. _____ I don't like *skiing*.

6. _____ Do you prefer *jogging* or tennis?

7. _____ The *laughing* clown was very funny.

8. _____ We've been *driving* all day.

9. _____ The *beginning* of the story was quite sad.

10. _____ He was arrested for *speeding*.

Unit 14

Relative Pronouns

Relative pronouns are used to link two sentences that have the same noun or pronoun in them. Relative pronouns form the beginning of a *relative clause*. In English there are five basic relative pronoun forms:

that = used when referring to either an animate or inanimate noun

who = used when referring to an animate noun

which = used when referring to an inanimate noun

whose = used as a possessive

elliptical relative pronoun = occurs when the relative pronoun is omitted

The noun in the introductory clause is called the *antecedent*. A relative pronoun replaces the noun in the second clause—the relative clause.

Let's look at how relative pronouns connect two sentences. If the same noun or pronoun is found in both sentences, the second one can be omitted and replaced by a relative pronoun. Then the two sentences are stated as one. Notice how the animate and inanimate nouns change to relative pronouns.

Two Sentences: He likes *the girl. The girl* comes from Alaska.
Relative Clause: He likes the girl *who comes from Alaska.* **OR** He likes the girl *that comes from Alaska.*

Two Sentences: I bought *the car. The car* needs repairs.
Relative Clause: I bought the car *that needs repairs.* **OR** I bought the car *which needs repairs.*

Nouns can be used as subjects, direct objects, indirect objects, objects of prepositions, and possessives; so, too, can relative pronouns that replace them.

There are specific uses for *that, who,* and *which;* however, in casual speech the relative pronoun *that* can be substituted for *who* or *which* except when the relative pronoun shows possession. Look at these examples with inanimate nouns:

Use in a Sentence	Pairs of Sentences	Relative Clauses Formed
subject	I found the money. The *money* was lost.	I found the money that was lost. I found the money which was lost.
direct object	I found the money. Bree lost the *money.*	I found the money that Bree lost. I found the money which Bree lost.
indirect object	N/A	N/A
preposition	I found the money. They spoke *about the money.*	I found the money that they spoke about. I found the money about which they spoke.
possessive	I found the money. The color *of* the money is green.	I found the money the color of which is green.

It is possible to substitute *whose* for a prepositional phrase starting with *of* with inanimate objects: *I found the money whose color is green.*

Now look at similar examples with animate nouns:

Use in a Sentence	Pairs of Sentences	Relative Clauses Formed
subject	I found the boy. The *boy* was lost.	I found the boy that was lost. I found the boy who was lost.
direct object	I found the boy. Kim met the *boy.*	I found the boy that Kim met. I found the boy whom Kim met.
indirect object	I found the boy. They gave the *boy* a gift.	I found the boy that they gave a gift to. I found the boy to whom they gave a gift.
preposition	I found the boy. They spoke *about the boy.*	I found the boy that they spoke about. I found the boy about whom they spoke.
possessive	I found the boy. The *boy's* father is a soldier.	I found the boy whose father is a soldier.

Careful! If *whom* or *which* is part of a prepositional phrase, the preposition can stand in front of *whom* or *which,* or it can stand at the end of the relative clause:

> I like the man *for whom* I work.
> I like the man *whom* I work for.

> These are the books *about which* she spoke.
> These are the books *which* she spoke *about.*

When the relative pronoun is *that*, the preposition always stands at the end of the relative clause:

> I like the man *that* I work *for.*
> These are the books *that* she spoke *about.*

When an indirect object noun is changed to a relative pronoun, the preposition *to* or *for* should be added to give the meaning of the original sentence. Examples:

> Do you know the man? I gave the man ten dollars.
> Do you know the man *to whom* I gave ten dollars?

> Andre saw the girl. I bought the girl some flowers.
> Andre saw the girl *that* I bought some flowers *for.*

If the relative pronoun is used as a direct object or object of a preposition, it can be omitted. It is then called *elliptical.* If a preposition is involved, it must stand at the end of the relative clause.

Usage	Relative Pronoun Used	Elliptical Relative Pronoun
direct object	He's the man that I met in Canada.	He's the man I met in Canada.
preposition	Where's the car in which she was sitting?	Where's the car she was sitting in?

Note: You should be aware that in casual speech many English speakers regularly substitute *who* for *whom.*

There are two types of relative clauses: *restrictive clauses* and *nonrestrictive clauses.* Restrictive relative clauses contain information that is essential to the meaning of the sentence. If that information is omitted, the sentence cannot be understood as intended. The restrictive relative clause identifies the person or thing talked about in the other clause. Here are two examples:

> The woman who stole the ring was soon arrested. (*who stole the ring* is essential information)
> What's the make of the car that you bought? (*that you bought* is essential information)

Nonrestrictive relative clauses merely give additional information but do not define the person or thing talked about in the other clause. The relative pronoun *that* should not be used in nonrestrictive relative clauses. However, in casual speech there is often substitution between *that* and the relative pronouns *who* and *which.* Here are two examples of nonrestrictive clauses:

> The mayor, who is out of town right now, will give a speech on Friday. (*who is out of town right now* is additional but nonessential information)
> The play, which lasted over three hours, was given rave reviews. (*which lasted over three hours* is additional but nonessential information)

Commas are used to separate a nonrestrictive relative clause from the other clause in the sentence.

exercise	14-1

Combine the following sentences by changing the second sentence to a relative clause. Use that *as the relative pronoun.*

1. I found the money. The money belonged to Jack.

   _____

2. She has a good memory. Her memory always serves her well.

   _____

3. This is the woman. I told you about the woman.

   _____

4. I have a document. The document proves my innocence.

   _____

5. They want to visit the country. Marsha comes from the country.

   _____

Follow the same directions. Use who, whom, *or* whose *as the relative pronoun.*

6. This is the doctor. The doctor saved my life.

   _____

7. Do you know the musician? I met the musician in Hawaii.

   _____

8. She likes the gentleman. I was telling her about the gentleman.

   _____

9. I visited the sisters. The sisters' father had recently died.

   _____

10. Jerod noticed the stranger. All the neighbors were staring at the stranger.

    _____

Follow the same directions. Use which *as the relative pronoun.*

11. Pablo threw away the picture. The boys had found the picture.

_____

12. I live in the house. My grandfather was born in the house.

_____

13. He bought a suit. The suit is navy blue.

_____

14. Anna has a new hat. I like the new hat very much.

_____

15. He wanted to paint the bench. A man was sitting on the bench.

_____

exercise 14-2

Complete each sentence with any appropriate phrase.

1. This is the lady about whom _____.

2. We visited a country that _____.

3. I don't like the people whom _____.

4. Where's the basket in which _____?

5. Peter laughed at the story that _____.

6. My aunt met the writer whom _____ about.

7. Sammie spoke with the teacher whose _____.

8. I met the manager whom _____ for.

9. She hates the blouse that _____.

10. Tell me about the tourists whose _____.

exercise	14-3

Rewrite each sentence, changing the relative clause to its elliptical form. Omit the relative pronoun.

> EXAMPLE: She's the girl whom I met there.
> *She's the girl I met there.*

1. He was in the city that I visited last year.

   _____

2. Did you finally meet the woman about whom I was telling you?

   _____

3. Ron sold the house that he was born in.

   _____

4. My father lost the checkbook that he kept his credit card in.

   _____

5. Did you find the ball that I threw over the fence?

   _____

6. That's the pretty girl for whom I wrote this poem.

   _____

7. I don't know the people whom he gave the flowers to.

   _____

8. The hat from which the magician pulled a white rabbit was empty.

   _____

9. She forgot the tickets that she had placed next to her briefcase.

   _____

10. They live in a tiny village, which we finally located on a map.

    _____

Reflexive Pronouns

Reflexive pronouns reflect back to the subject of a sentence. The English reflexive pronouns are: *myself, yourself, himself, herself, itself, ourselves, yourselves,* and *themselves.* Each one can only be used with its personal pronoun counterpart when that personal pronoun is the subject of the sentence:

Personal Pronoun	Reflexive Pronoun	A Sample Sentence
I	myself	I hurt myself again.
you	yourself	You can do it yourself.
he	himself	He enjoyed himself.
she	herself	She helped herself to some candy.
it	itself	It destroyed itself in a few seconds.
we	ourselves	We found ourselves in a strange city.
you	yourselves	You must clean yourselves up before dinner.
they	themselves	They accidentally burned themselves.

If the reflexive pronoun and the personal pronoun are not counterparts, then personal pronouns should be used in the sentence. Look at these examples:

Counterparts	Not Counterparts
I hurt myself again.	I hurt him again. I hurt them again.
He enjoyed himself.	He enjoyed it. He enjoyed them.
They harmed themselves.	They harmed me. They harmed her.

Remember that third-person singular and plural nouns will use the appropriate third-person singular and plural reflexive pronouns:

Marta bought herself a new car.
The boy cut himself.
The alien creature wounded itself with its own claws.
The men helped themselves to some beer.

| exercise | 15-1 |

Rewrite each sentence appropriately with the subject personal pronouns given. Change to the appropriate reflexive pronoun.

1. I found myself in a difficult situation.

    You (sing.) _____.

    He _____.

    She _____.

    We _____.

    They _____.

    Amy _____.

2. We enjoyed ourselves at the party.

    I _____.

    You (pl.) _____.

    He _____.

    She _____.

    They _____.

    The boys _____.

3. He is going to be very proud of himself.

    I _____.

    My friends _____.

    Mother _____.

    They _____.

    We _____.

    Abdul and Ricky _____.

4. I just couldn't help myself.

    You (pl.) _____.

He _____.

She _____.

We _____.

They _____.

The men _____.

---

exercise   **15-2**

Replace the object personal pronoun in each sentence with the appropriate reflexive pronoun.

1. Jerry liked me in the new suit.

   _____

2. They busied her with several different tasks.

   _____

3. We were very proud of them.

   _____

4. She is buying us a few new outfits.

   _____

5. The children hurt me.

   _____

6. I have to ask him what to do now.

   _____

7. The young woman told you not to give in.

   _____

8. He wants to find me something nice to wear.

   _____

9. You've harmed no one but us.

   _____

10. The lizard hid them under a rock.

   _____

Possession

Nouns form **the possessive** in two ways: (1) they become the object of the preposition *of,* or (2) they add the ending -*'s* (apostrophe plus -*s*). Look at these examples:

the roar of a lion	a lion's roar
the color of the book	the book's color
the children of Mrs. Diaz	Mrs. Diaz's children
the prey of the wolves	the wolves' prey

(See Unit 12 regarding punctuation to review the rules for using the apostrophe.)

The possessive is used to show to whom or to what something belongs:

This is *Ginny's* car.
The kittens *of an alley cat* have a hard life.

exercise	16-1

Change the italicized possessive phrase to a possessive ending in -'s.

> EXAMPLE: The color of the car is red.
> *The car's color is red.*

1. The center *of the storm* was just north of the city.

   _____

2. The condition *of the victims* was very serious.

   _____

3. I don't understand the behavior *of my classmates.*

   _____

4. The equipment *of the lab* was outdated.

_____

5. The efforts *of each man* helped to make the project a success.

_____

6. The many illnesses *of the animals* were evidence of the filthy conditions.

_____

7. The documents *of the young lawyer* were very impressive.

_____

8. The room was filled with the scent *of the roses.*

_____

9. A hunter captured the mother *of the little bear cub.*

_____

10. We drove to the northern border *of the town.*

_____

Unit 17

Possessive Pronouns

Possessive pronouns are sometimes called *possessive adjectives*. No matter what you call them, their use is clear and simple. Just like reflexive pronouns, possessive pronouns have personal pronoun counterparts. Look at this table of pronouns to see the relationship:

Subject	Object	Possessive 1	Possessive 2
I	me	my	mine
you	you	your	yours
he	him	his	his
she	her	her	hers
it	it	its	its
we	us	our	ours
they	them	their	theirs

There is a difference in the use of the possessive pronouns 1 and 2. The possessive pronoun 1 always stands before a noun and modifies it. The possessive pronoun 2 replaces a possessive pronoun 1 and a noun, when the noun is understood. Look at these examples:

My gift is unusual.	Which gift is *mine?* (my gift)
Is this *your* brother?	The seat on the right will be *yours.* (your seat)
Our friends live here.	These two dogs are *ours.* (our dogs)
His aunt is a doctor.	*His* is a doctor. (his aunt)
Her dress is very nice.	*Hers* is very nice. (her dress)

Possessive pronouns tell to whom or to what something belongs.

exercise | **17-1**

Change the possessive pronoun 1 to a possessive pronoun 2 and omit the noun.

EXAMPLE: She has my book.
She has mine.

1. The car on the corner is my car.

   _____

2. Was this your house?

   _____

3. The invading soldiers searched their house.

   _____

4. Did Dee find her briefcase?

   _____

5. Our relatives have lived in Brazil for a long time.

   _____

6. His boss is fair with everyone.

   _____

7. These problems are entirely his problems.

   _____

8. I need your advice.

   _____

9. My landlord is going to raise the rent.

   _____

10. Their long conversations made no sense.

    _____

exercise	17-2

Change the italicized word or phrase to the possessive pronoun counterpart of the subject of the sentence.

> EXAMPLE: He likes *the* new car.
> *He likes his new car.*

1. The women want to visit *some* relatives in Europe.

    _____

2. She takes *the* children for a long walk.

    _____

3. Do you have *the* tools in the truck?

    _____

4. I sent *the* address and telephone number to the office.

    _____

5. We want *this one.*

    _____

6. The picture fell out of *the* frame.

    _____

7. They spend *a lot of* time in Canada.

    _____

8. Are you selling *these?*

    _____

9. I left some papers in *the* apartment.

    _____

10. Jose found *the* wallet under the bed.

    _____

exercise	17-3

Circle the boldface word that best completes each sentence.

1. Did you leave **yours/mine/your** keys on the desk?

2. Her brother met **his/her/their** wife in Paris.

3. This book is **our/his/her**, and that one belongs to Smita.

4. Where did they buy **theirs/blouse/its**?

5. I believe I forgot **mine/her/my** again.

6. My sister gave **mine/her/its** watch to me.

7. I saw your tickets, but where are **her/my/ours**?

8. **Hers/Theirs/His** uncle is coming to America to live.

9. The fox hurt **its/hers/front** foot in a trap.

10. May I have **hers/my/mine** dinner now?

Prepositions

A **preposition** connects a certain word in a sentence to a noun or pronoun. But the meaning of prepositional phrases (preposition followed by a noun or pronoun) is varied. They tell where, when, why, how, or whose. Look at these examples:

where = in the garden

when = until Monday

why = because of the bad weather

how = by train

whose = of the bride

Here is a list of some commonly used prepositions.

about	behind	for	since
above	below	from	through
across	beside	in	to
after	between	of	under
along	by	off	until
around	despite	on	up
at	down	out	with
before	during	over	without

Compound prepositions consist of more than one word: *along with, because of, due to, in spite of, on account of, next to, on top of, together with,* and so on.

When a noun is used in a prepositional phrase, it does not change. But most pronouns do:

I → with me	we → from us
you → to you	they → for them
he → by him	the boys → to the boys
she → without her	a girl → after a girl
it → on it	my keys → over my keys

exercise   18-1

Change the noun phrase in the prepositional phrase to the appropriate pronoun. Keep the same number and gender.

1. The man next to Jordan is a senator.

   _____

2. Did they leave after the play?

   _____

3. Evan was dancing with his aunt.

   _____

4. Why did you leave the house without your wallet?

   _____

5. Are there washers and dryers in the apartments?

   _____

6. Juan had some nice wine for his guests.

   _____

7. The man with Yvette is her new boyfriend.

   _____

8. A large bear was coming toward the man.

   _____

9. The letter from my parents made me very happy.

   _____

10. In spite of all her problems, Tonya went on smiling.

   _____

Note: Sometimes a prepositional phrase connected to the subject of a sentence can cause confusion. This is especially true when one of those elements is singular and the other is plural. Always remember that the subject—not the prepositional phrase—determines the form of the verb.

Singular Subject + Plural Object of the Preposition
The box of fresh cookies *was* torn open by their dog.
Each of you *has* a duty to help them.
One of the youngest candidates *needs* a lot more money.

Plural Subject + Singular Object of the Preposition
The musicians in the little band *were* given a new contract.
Several girls from our school *have* been awarded scholarships.

exercise   18-2

Circle the boldface word that best completes each sentence.

1. One of the boys **are/is/were** a friend of mine.

2. The **woman/person/women** from our church are having a bake sale.

3. Each of the people at these meetings **want/have to/needs** to know the truth.

4. The box of chocolates **was/are/were** a gift from Thomas.

5. The students in this class **need/wants/has** more time to prepare.

6. Every one of you on the team **want/has/have** the chance to be a champion.

7. The magician, together with his assistants, **makes/are making/make** the rabbits disappear.

8. All of you in the third row **needs/need/was needed** to stand up.

9. Many tourists on this flight **doesn't/don't/does** have the proper visa.

10. A young teacher, along with several of her pupils, **find/are locating/captures** the robber.

Capitalization

You are already aware that nouns fall into two general categories: proper nouns and common nouns. All nouns refer to persons, places, things, or ideas, but only certain nouns—proper nouns—are capitalized. All other nouns do not require capitalization (unless they occur at the beginning of a sentence). Let's look at the specifics that govern English **capitalization**.

A. The first word in a sentence is always capitalized. It does not matter if the sentence begins with a common noun or some other grammatical element.

> Terrell is my brother.
> The children are fast asleep.
> Are you going home now?
> When is that program on?

B. The first word in the title of any work of art (e.g., short story, article, book, TV program, film, painting, song, CD) is always capitalized. All the other words in the title are also capitalized, except for the articles, conjunctions, and prepositions. (However, if an article, conjunction, or preposition is the last word in a title, it must be capitalized.)

> "How to Buy a House"
> *The Adventures of Tom Sawyer*
> *Finding Nemo*
> "Take Me Out to the Ball Game"

C. The same rule applies to official names of businesses and institutions.

> The University of Illinois at Chicago
> Sears Roebuck and Company

D. First names, last names, initials, and personal titles of all kinds are always capitalized.

> Jason Kensington
> Ms. Alicia Jones
> Professor Rosa Morena
> Senator William Hayes
> General Dwight D. Eisenhower
> J. D. Powers

E. Titles that are not part of directly addressing the person who bears the title should not be capitalized. Compare the following:

> I met a senator at the meeting.   Hello, Senator. How are you?
> Is she the governor now?   It's good to see you, Governor Bejcek.
> A captain entered the room.   Please sit down, Captain Bligh.

F. All days of the week, months of the year, and holidays are capitalized. Seasons and other categories of time are not.

> Is it Monday already?   The weather is cooler in the fall.
> My favorite month is June.   Where do you spend the winter?
> She was born March 3, 2001.   How many years are in a decade?
> Today is the Fourth of July.   The twentieth century was important.
> I like Halloween.   It's a new millennium.

G. There are special rules for abbreviations for time. *B.C.* and *A.D.* are always capitalized. *B.C.* is used for eras or years that occurred *before Christ. A.D.* is used for eras or years that occurred *anno Domini* ("in the year of our Lord"), that is, beginning with the first year after Christ's birth. (B.C. follows the date; A.D. precedes the date.) *A.M.* and *P.M.* may or may not be capitalized. *A.M.* refers to the hours between midnight and noon, and *P.M.* refers to the hours between noon and midnight.

> That happened in the fifth century B.C.
> Columbus first landed in the New World in A.D. 1492.
> They arrived exactly at 9:00 P.M.
> I set my alarm for 7:35 A.M.

exercise   19-1

Rewrite the words in each sentence that require capitalization.

1. john bought a new cadillac for his wife.

   _____

2. is colonel brubaker a friend of governor dassoff?

   _____

3. the president of the company was born on march tenth in the city of buffalo.

   _____

4. we stopped at a restaurant in chicago and ordered southern fried chicken.

   _____

5. in the summer the kids from whittier school play baseball at st. james park.

   _____

6. she invested some money last february with e. f. hutton in new york.

   _____

7. ms. assad met the general while he was touring the northern part of texas.

   _____

8. are mr. and mrs. cermak planning a large wedding for their daughter, britney?

   _____

9. ted bought us a coke and a hot dog for lunch.

   _____

10. the students read *the adventures of huckleberry finn* in school last may.

    _____

11. his sister was born on may tenth in cleveland memorial hospital.

    _____

12. mia got up at precisely eight o'clock a.m.

    _____

13. do you know the president of the corporation?

    _____

14. if you see mayor yamamoto, tell him the governor has phoned again.

    _____

15. we get the new york times every day but sunday.

    _____

exercise **19-2**

Rewrite the following dates with the numbers shown as words. The order of the numbers corresponds to month/day/year.

1. 5/10/1865 _____

2. 11/11/1918 _____

3. 7/4/1776 _____

4. 12/24/2000 _____

5. 1/1/1999 _____

Rewrite the following times as words and add A.M. or P.M. Look at the phrase in parentheses to help you decide which one.

6. 9:00 (in the morning) _____

7. 11:30 (in the evening) _____

8. 6:45 (at dawn) _____

9. 7:50 (at sunset) _____

10. 8:15 (during breakfast) _____

Unit 20

Comparative and Superlative Forms

The **comparative** of an adjective or adverb describes a comparison of one person or thing with another person or thing. Most comparatives require an *-er* ending, for example, *taller, shallower*. If the adjective or adverb ends in a single consonant, that consonant is doubled before adding the ending: *mad → madder*. If an adjective or adverb ends in *-y*, change it to *-i* then add *-er*: *funny → funnier*.

The **superlative** of an adjective or adverb shows the greatest degree of the meaning of the adjective or adverb. Most superlatives end in *-est*: *tallest, shallowest*. If the adjective or adverb ends in a single consonant, that consonant is doubled before adding the ending: *mad → maddest*. If an adjective or adverb ends in *-y*, change it to *-i* then add *-est*: *funny → funniest*.

Both the comparative and the superlative are formed in another way by using *more* or *most*. The word *more* is placed in front of the adjective or adverb to form the comparative, and the word *most* is placed in front of the adjective or adverb to form the superlative: *more interesting/most interesting, more logical/most logical*. This formation is used primarily with words that are of two syllables or more and that come to English from French, Latin, or other foreign sources.

The other formation (*long, longer, longest*) is Anglo-Saxon in origin. Compare these lists of comparatives and superlatives:

Anglo-Saxon Origin		Foreign Origin	
bigger	biggest	more critical	most critical
finer	finest	more dangerous	most dangerous
grander	grandest	more dynamic	most dynamic
happier	happiest	more fruitful	most fruitful
jollier	jolliest	more harmonious	most harmonious
kinder	kindest	more hopeless	most hopeless
mightier	mightiest	more intense	most intense
poorer	poorest	more sensitive	most sensitive
smaller	smallest	more visible	most visible
thinner	thinnest	more willing	most willing

Note that words that end in *-ful*, *-less*, and *-ing* use *more* and *most* to form the comparative and superlative, even though such words do not have a foreign language origin.

There are a few irregular formations that must simply be memorized:

Positive	Comparative	Superlative
bad	worse	worst
far	farther/further	farthest/furthest
good	better	best
little (amount)	less	least
many	more	most
much	more	most
well	better	best

It is possible to use a comparative in a sentence without mentioning the person or thing with which another person or thing is being compared. Look at these examples:

Jorge is a lot *taller*.
My sister was *thinner* a few years ago.

In such sentences the person or thing compared is assumed. When stating the person or thing with which another person or thing is being compared, use the word *than*:

Jorge is a lot taller *than* Michelle.
My sister was thinner a few years ago *than* she is now.

The formation of both adjectives and adverbs in the comparative is identical. The difference is how they are used in a sentence:

My car is faster than your car. (adjective)
She runs faster than you do. (adverb)

With adverbs that end in *-ly,* both forms of comparative and superlative are possible:

He spoke *quicker*./He spoke *more quickly*.
He spoke *the quickest*./He spoke *the most quickly*.

The superlative adjective or adverb frequently is preceded by the word *the*:

Lars is *the* strongest boy.
She is *the* most beautiful girl here.

When the superlative is a predicative adjective and not followed by a noun, the word *the* can be omitted:

Lars is strongest when he's not tired.
She is most beautiful when she wakes up in the morning.

Comparative and superlative adverbs that are formed with *more* and *most* require the adverbial ending *-ly*:

more willingly
most capably

exercise 20-1

Rewrite each sentence with the italicized word changed to the comparative.

1. This freight train is moving *slowly*.

   _____

2. My *young* brother is a mathematician.

   _____

3. Where is the *old* man you told me about?

   _____

4. Fanny swims *well*, but she still cannot dive.

   _____

5. Hunter's cold is *bad* today.

   _____

6. They have *much* to do before the end of the day.

   _____

7. I think Robbie is *intelligent*.

   _____

8. The new employee is *careless* about his work.

   _____

9. She has *many* friends in the city.

   _____

10. This project is *critical* to the success of the company.

    _____

11. Clarice just can't speak *quietly*.

    _____

12. We have a *big* house out in the country.

    _____

13. Do you think that kind of language is *sinful?*

    _____

14. The inn is *far* down this road.

_____

15. Your friend is *reckless*.

_____

exercise	20-2

Use each set of words to write a sentence. Make a comparison using than. *(You may use different forms of the words listed.)*

      EXAMPLE: Maurice/Ingrid/speak/loudly
              Maurice speaks louder than Ingrid.

1. cats/dogs/run/fast

_____

2. my brother/your sister/write/beautiful

_____

3. you/I/learn/quick

_____

4. Rashad/Steven/sell/many cars

_____

5. New York/Chicago/big

_____

6. Ginger/Fred/dance/well

_____

7. lake/sky/look/blue

_____

8. our team/your team/play/capable

_____

9. the husband/the wife/seem/jealous

_____

10. Mr. Espinosa/Ms. VanDam/have/little money

_____

exercise   20-3

Rewrite each sentence with the italicized word changed to the superlative.

1. Carlos is the *short* boy in the last row.

   _____

2. Paris is *beautiful.*

   _____

3. The white stallion runs *fast.*

   _____

4. Is Russia a *large* country in Europe?

   _____

5. Is this an *interesting* article?

   _____

6. They say that the CEO is *rich.*

   _____

7. Smoking is *bad* for your health.

   _____

8. The soprano sings *softly.*

   _____

9. The vice president spoke *brilliantly.*

   _____

10. Is the planet Pluto *far?*

    _____

11. Larry gets up *early.*

    _____

12. She is *systematic* about everything she does.

    _____

13. Brian is a *cute* boy.

    _____

14. Laura plays the violin *well.*

_____

15. That book is *boring.*

_____

exercise   20-4

Rewrite the words as a sentence. Form the adjective or adverb as a superlative and add any necessary words.

    EXAMPLE: Dennis/jump/high
           Dennis jumps the highest.

1. Melanie/funny/girl/in class

_____

2. what/distant/planet

_____

3. your/handwriting/bad

_____

4. men/at the party/eat/much

_____

5. Olive/smart/all/girls/in school

_____

6. Mozart/compose/beautiful/music

_____

7. grandmother/bake/delicious/cakes

_____

8. pickpocket/steal/many/wallets

_____

9. Raj/think/this symphony/boring

_____

10. Janice/my/good/friend

_____

| exercise | 20-5 |

Rewrite each sentence twice, first changing the adjective or adverb to the comparative and then to the superlative.

1. My coffee is hot.

   _____

   _____

2. Is this math problem difficult?

   _____

   _____

3. I feel well today.

   _____

   _____

4. Life in the jungle is dangerous.

   _____

   _____

5. This village is poor.

   _____

   _____

6. Mr. Hong always has little time.

   _____

   _____

7. The choir sang a merry song.

   _____

   _____

8. She wore a shabby dress.

   _____

   _____

9. Bert has many friends.

   _____

   _____

10. She can speak calmly about it.

    _____

    _____

Conjunctions

Conjunctions join words, phrases, and sentences together. First, let's look at some of the commonly used *coordinating conjunctions*: *and, but, or, nor, for, so,* and *yet*. Notice how they can combine words, phrases, or complete sentences:

Combined Words	Combined Phrases	Combined Sentences
"Don *or* Norma" "meat *and* potatoes"	"healthy again *yet* unable to work"	"We remained by the fire, *but* Lance went to the park to skate."

Correlative conjunctions are also important. They consist of a pair of words that appear in different parts of the same sentence. The most commonly used are *both . . . and, either . . . or, neither . . . nor,* and *not only . . . but also* (sometimes stated as *not only . . . also*). Examples:

Both Yoko *and* Marco have problems.
Either you work hard *or* you leave.
Neither the boys *nor* the girls wanted to end the game.
You are *not only* a poor loser *but also* a bad soccer player.

Dependent (or subordinating) clauses consist of a subject and a verb. But these clauses usually cannot stand alone. Dependent clauses are preceded by *subordinating conjunctions* and are combined with an independent clause. The list of subordinating conjunctions is long. Here are some of the most commonly used:

after	before	since	until
although	even though	so that	when
as if	how	than	whenever
as long as	if	that	where
as though	now that	though	wherever
because	once	unless	while

Let's look at some example sentences:

> *After* she arrived, Alberto was the first to greet her.
> *Although* he was tired, he continued to run.
> I just don't know *how* you do it.
> *If* you don't pay your rent, you'll have to move.
> Bob doesn't know *where* she lives.

exercise	21-1

Combine each pair of sentences with the appropriate coordinating conjunction: and, but, or, nor, for, so, *or* yet.

1. That's my brother. The woman next to him is his wife.

   _____

2. We ran into the tent. Our clothes were already soaked by the storm.

   _____

3. Should we watch TV tonight? Should we go see a movie?

   _____

4. She began to cry. The book ended so sadly.

   _____

5. I hurried as fast as I could. I arrived home late as usual.

   _____

6. The red car was already sold. Kim bought the blue one.

   _____

7. Our dog likes to play in the yard. Our cat prefers to stay in the house.

   _____

8. Milo lives on Oak Street. His brother lives nearby.

   _____

9. Their credit was very poor. They decided to buy a piano anyway.

   _____

10. I love the snowy beauty of winter. I hate the heat of summer.

   _____

exercise	21-2

Fill in the blanks with the appropriate correlative conjunctions: both . . . and, either . . . or, neither . . . nor, *or* not only . . . but also.

1. _____ Maribeth _____ I will ever visit them again.

2. I want to buy _____ a new blouse _____ a new skirt.

3. They were already introduced to _____ Carol _____ her mother.

4. You _____ work too little _____ spend too much money.

5. _____ Father _____ Mother became ill during the cruise.

6. She wants _____ your help _____ your advice.

7. Reggie _____ broke his leg _____ bruised both arms.

8. It's always _____ too hot _____ too cold for you.

9. _____ the kitchen _____ the bathroom need to be cleaned.

10. _____ Cary _____ Kelly showed up at the party.

exercise	21-3

Complete each sentence with a dependent clause to follow each subordinating conjunction.

1. She left for home after _____.

2. When _____, Pedro started to laugh.

3. I won't help you unless _____.

4. Do you know where _____?

5. Once _____, I was able to relax.

6. Chris closed the book before _____.

7. You can stay up late as long as _____.

8. While _____, he relaxed under a tree.

9. I don't remember if _____.

10. Now that _____, they often go to the theater.

exercise	21-4

Write two original sentences with each of the following conjunctions.

1. but _____

_____

2. unless _____

_____

3. neither . . . nor _____

_____

4. where _____

_____

5. how _____

_____

6. and _____

_____

7. not only . . . but also _____

_____

8. for _____

_____

9. when _____

_____

10. either . . . or _____

_____

Interrogatives

Interrogatives are words that ask a question. They are placed at (or near) the beginning of the sentence, and that sentence ends with a question mark. Some interrogatives are pronouns: *who, whom, whose, what,* and *which.* They can act as:

- the subject of a sentence
- a direct object
- the object of a preposition
- a possessive

Look at these examples:

Subject: Who is standing on the corner?

Whose is for sale? (The noun subject is understood.)

What needs to be done?

Which is for me?

Direct object: Whom did you see last night?

Whose did you borrow? (The noun object is understood.)

What will they do?

Which have you selected?

Preposition: With whom was she dancing?

About whose was he speaking? (The noun is understood.)

To what are you referring?

In which is it located?

Possessive: Whose house burned down? (*Whose* modifies *house.*)

Other interrogatives act as adverbs: *how, when, where,* and *why.* Some examples:

Question	Possible Answer
How did he walk?	slowly
When was the party?	on Tuesday
Where are you going?	to the store
Why are you limping?	because my foot hurts

There are also some commonly used phrases that are a combination of *what, which,* and *how* and other words. Questions are formed with them like with other interrogatives:

> what brand of, what kind of, what sort of, what about
> which one, which way, which part of, which of you
> how much, how many, how often, how about

Of course, these are not the only such combinations. They are examples. You will discover others that are formed similarly. Some example sentences:

> What kind of dress do you want to buy?
> What about your brother?
> Which one is for me?
> Which of you will help me?

Interrogative words can be used as conjunctions to combine two clauses. You encountered some of them in Unit 21 on conjunctions. But be careful! The sentence formed by using an interrogative as a conjunction is not necessarily a question when combined with another clause. It depends upon whether you are asking a question or making a statement:

Question	Statement
Do you know who he is?	Jill told me who he is.
Does she understand how it works?	I can't explain how it works.
Who told you where it was?	They couldn't discover where it was.
Can you tell me what kind of car this is?	I don't know what kind of car this is.

Notice the change in word order between a direct question and an interrogative clause combined with another clause. In direct questions the verb precedes the subject. In an interrogative clause the verb follows the subject.

Who *are* these people?	She asked me who these people *are.*
When *did* they *arrive?*	I don't know when they *arrived.*
How far *can* he *swim?*	They ask how far he *can swim.*

exercise	22-1

Look at the italicized word or words in each sentence. Then, using the appropriate interrogative word, ask the question that relates to that word.

> EXAMPLE: *Thomas* is a friend of his.
> *Who is a friend of his?*

1. Lupita bought *a black* dress.

   _____

2. Panama is located *in Central America.*

   _____

3. She wanted to buy *a new hat and coat.*

   _____

4. Kevin decided to go *home.*

   _____

5. Kendall spent a lot of time talking *with his cousin.*

   _____

6. She started to laugh *because the movie was so funny.*

   _____

7. The man on crutches came down the steps *carefully.*

   _____

8. The clock stopped *at precisely 10:42 A.M.*

   _____

9. *Ms. Ewell* has worked for this company for years.

   _____

10. *My sister's* husband is a firefighter.

    _____

11. She should select *this* pair of gloves.

    _____

12. There are *more than fifteen* people in the room.

    _____

13. This dog is *a Chihuahua.*

_____

14. *The lion's presence* meant danger.

_____

15. Los Angeles is *either north or south* from here.

_____

exercise	22-2

Circle the boldface word or phrase that best answers the question.

1. Whose car is in the driveway? **your/the girl/Nikki's**

2. What's crawling on the wall? **there/a bug/their house**

3. When can you pick the children up? **tomorrow/here/at your house**

4. What brand of car did you buy? **a Ford/foreign/a new one**

5. Which one of them took the money? **him/that man/theirs**

6. How long is this plank? **several/more than one/six feet**

7. Whom did he visit in Mexico? **the ocean/mountains/a friend**

8. Where is the village you come from? **for many people/near the sea/a little earlier**

9. How does your aunt feel today? **always/quickly/better**

10. Which part of the play didn't you understand? **the ending/of the actors/at the theater**

exercise	22-3

Complete each sentence with any appropriate phrase.

1. I don't know why _____.

2. With whom were you _____?

3. He won't explain what kind of _____.

4. Whose parents _____?

5. What sort of man would _____?

6. Andi told me what _____ .

7. It's hard to believe how _____ .

8. The accident happened when _____ .

9. How much _____ ?

10. Which one of you _____ ?

Negation

No is the opposite of *yes*. It is used as a negative response to a question. But there are other negative forms in English as well.

Simple **negation** occurs by placing *not* after the conjugated verb in a sentence. It is important to remember that it is the conjugated verb that determines the location of *not* and not the other verbal forms that may also be in a sentence.

> He is *not* at home today.
> We do *not* want to buy a car at this time.
> Marianne has *not* responded to my letter.

If the sentence is in the form of a question, *not* stands behind the subject:

> Can you *not* understand?
> How could he *not* have helped us?
> Will Martin *not* share his good fortune?

But in the case of a contraction with *not*, the two parts of the contraction are never separated. This is true whether the sentence is a statement or a question:

> He *isn't* at home today.   *Can't* you understand?
> We *don't* want to buy a car.   Why *couldn't* he help us?
> She *hasn't* answered yet.   *Won't* Martin share with us?

If the negated verb is not *to be, to have,* or other auxiliary (*can, should, must,* etc.), the negation is formed from the present or past tense of *do,* depending upon the tense of the verb:

> I am not   I do not speak
> she has not   she doesn't learn
> you shouldn't   you did not understand
> he can't   he didn't worry

Certain other negative words have two forms. One form begins with *no-* (except for *never* and *neither*), and the other consists of *not* followed by another word. When these words are not negative, they have a special positive form that often uses the word *some.* Look at the varieties that exist:

115

Formed with *no-*	Formed with *not*	Positive Form
none	not any	some
no one	not anyone (or anybody)	someone (or somebody)
nothing	not anything	something
nowhere	not anywhere	somewhere
never*	not ever	ever
neither*	not either	either

Take note of the spelling.

Be aware of how the two forms are used differently:

I have *none* to give you.	I do *not* have *anything* to give you.
He spoke to *no one*.	He did *not* speak to *anyone*.
We want *nothing* from you.	We do *not* want *anything* from you.
She's *nowhere* to be found.	She's *not anywhere* to be found.
I'll *never* forgive you.	I will *not ever* forgive you.
He wants *neither* of them.	He does *not* want *either* of them.

When the negative word is removed from the sentence, the positive form replaces it:

Hector didn't dance with anyone. → Hector danced with someone.
The customer wants nothing. → The customer wants something.

Note: English never uses a double negative—for example, *doesn't want nothing*.

exercise 23-1

Rewrite each sentence twice, first by adding not, *then by using a contraction of* not.

1. The boys were playing basketball at the park.

   _____

   _____

2. My sister is a concert pianist.

   _____

   _____

3. Are you well?

   _____

   _____

4. His nephew is learning Japanese.

   _____

   _____

5. Can they explain how this happened?

_____

_____

6. The judge ordered him sent to prison.

_____

_____

7. We will be traveling to Spain this summer.

_____

_____

8. Does Mr. Amin have our lawnmower?

_____

_____

9. My sister spends a lot of time in the library.

_____

_____

10. Judith understood the situation.

_____

_____

exercise **23-2**

Rewrite each sentence by removing the negation. Use the appropriate positive form where necessary.

1. I haven't had enough time to work on this.

_____

2. Mark doesn't get to work on time.

_____

3. She didn't bring her dog along.

_____

4. Have you never been to New York City?

_____

5. Lin wasn't speaking with anyone.

    _____

6. The children don't cooperate with the substitute teacher.

    _____

7. They don't live anywhere in the city.

    _____

8. Couldn't the horse run faster?

    _____

9. Marta didn't break the window.

    _____

10. No, I don't like this kind of music.

    _____

11. Chase isn't dancing with anyone.

    _____

12. Can't you find anything you need?

    _____

13. I haven't written the proposal for them.

    _____

14. No, she doesn't spend her vacation with us.

    _____

15. He got nothing interesting in the mail.

    _____

exercise   23-3

Write original sentences with the negative words in parentheses.

1. (not) _____

2. (never) _____

3. (no one) _____

4. (not anywhere) _____

5. (not anything) _____

6. (none) _____

7. (not ever) _____

8. (neither) _____

9. (nowhere) _____

10. (nothing) _____

Numbers

Numbers are generally used for specifying amounts and in mathematics: addition, subtraction, multiplication, and division. You have undoubtedly encountered them in many forms. Let's first review *cardinal numbers*:

0	zero	21	twenty-one
1	one	22	twenty-two
2	two	30	thirty
3	three	40	forty
4	four	50	fifty
5	five	60	sixty
6	six	70	seventy
7	seven	80	eighty
8	eight	90	ninety
9	nine	100	one hundred
10	ten	101	one hundred one
11	eleven	102	one hundred two
12	twelve	200	two hundred
13	thirteen	500	five hundred
14	fourteen	1,000	one thousand
15	fifteen	2,000	two thousand
16	sixteen	10,000	ten thousand
17	seventeen	11,000	eleven thousand
18	eighteen	20,000	twenty thousand
19	nineteen	100,000	one hundred thousand
20	twenty	111,111	one hundred eleven thousand one hundred eleven

Careful! English names for certain large numbers differ from those in other languages:

English	Number
million	1,000,000
billion	1,000,000,000
trillion	1,000,000,000,000

When numbers are used in equations, there are specific mathematical terms to be used. In addition, numbers are combined by either the word *plus* or the word *and*: five plus three, ten and nine.

In subtraction, the equation requires using the word *minus* (−): ten minus four.

In multiplication, the equation requires using the word *times* (×): six times three.

In division, the equation requires the phrase *divided by* (÷ or /): twenty divided by five.

If an equation has an equal sign (=) in it, it is stated as *equals* or *is*: two plus two equals four, six minus three is three.

If a number is a decimal, the decimal is expressed by the word *point*: 6.5 is said as "six point five"; 10.7 is said as "ten point seven."

The *ordinal numbers* are those that show a rank in a group or series. Most ordinals are formed by adding *-th* to the end of the number: *tenth, twentieth, sixty-seventh, hundredth,* and so on. But five ordinal numbers have special spellings which should be memorized:

1 = first
2 = second
3 = third
5 = fifth
12 = twelfth

Some example sentences with ordinal numbers:

We have three daughters, but Denise was our first.
The second seating for dinner is at 8:30 P.M.
She was born on the twenty-fifth of June.

Dates are expressed in two ways: *May fifth* or *the fifth of May*. When giving a date as a number, it is most common to give the month before the day: 9/11 = September eleventh, 6/12 = June twelfth. In many other languages, the day precedes the month. This can cause confusion, because to some people 6/12 means "the sixth of December." To English speakers it most commonly means "June twelfth." To avoid such confusion, it is wise to give dates in this form: June 12, 2005.

Ordinals are also used to express fractions other than ½:

½ = one-half (not an ordinal)
¼ = one-fourth (**Note:** One-fourth is sometimes expressed as "one-quarter" or "a quarter.")
⅓ = one-third
³⁄₁₀ = three-tenths
¹⁴⁄₂₅ = fourteen twenty-fifths (Notice the plural formation of the ordinal when the accompanying number is greater than one.)

Years that precede 2000 are expressed in two parts: 1850 is said as "eighteen fifty,"

1066 is said as "ten sixty-six." The years that follow 1999 are said another way:

2000	two thousand
2001	two thousand one, or twenty oh one
2002	two thousand two, or twenty oh two
2010	two thousand ten, or twenty ten
2022	two thousand twenty-two, or twenty twenty-two

When saying on what date an event occurred, the word *on* is optional:

The boy was born *on* May first.
The boy was born May first.

exercise   24-1

Rewrite each equation in words.

1. $5 + 7 = 12$

_____

2. $11 - 6 = 5$

_____

3. $345 - 220 = 125$

_____

4. $22 \times 10 = 220$

_____

5. $100 \times 63 = 6,300$

_____

6. $10,000 / 500 = 200$

_____

7. $880 \times 3 = 2,640$

_____

8. $88,000 - 55,000 = 33,000$

_____

9. $11.5 \times 10 = 115$

_____

10. $93.3 / 3 = 31.1$

_____

exercise	24-2

Change the cardinal number in parentheses to the appropriate ordinal number.

1. Mr. Woo was born on the (2) _____ of October.

2. I'm sitting in the (4) _____ row.

3. My birthday was on the (21) _____ of July.

4. This is only the (3) _____ time we met.

5. The old woman died on her (100) _____ birthday.

6. They're celebrating their (30) _____ anniversary.

7. Who's the (5) _____ boy in line?

8. That was her (10) _____ phone call today.

9. Mr. Burton was their (1,000) _____ customer and won a prize.

10. Adam scored in the (99) _____ percentile.

11. I think I was (1) _____ in line.

12. Our seats are in the (12) _____ row.

13. Christmas Day is always on the (25) _____.

14. The old woman died on her (86) _____ birthday.

15. Our new car arrived on the (22) _____ of August.

exercise	24-3

Complete each sentence with the date shown in parentheses written as words. In each case the month precedes the day (e.g., 5/2 = May second).

1. (8/10) She was born on _____.

2. (10/12) He'll arrive on _____.

3. (11/11) The party will be _____.

4. (2/16/1999) He died on _____.

5. (4/1/2002) They met on _____.

6. (12/24) Christmas Eve is ——————————————.

7. (7/4) Where will you spend ——————————————?

8. (1492) Columbus arrived in the New World in ——————————————.

9. (2/14/2004) The dance is ——————————————.

10. (6/2) Was the baby born on ——————————————?

Some Important Contrasts

As you study English and become more and more proficient, you will become aware that there are native speakers who say things that break the rules of good grammar. The more you know about English, the more you'll discover that this is true. Natives in all languages speak at different levels of competency. Some speak with great grammatical accuracy. Others are more casual or just careless and disregard the rules for good language.

The following eight pairs of words demonstrate where natives frequently make errors. By being aware of these words, you can make a choice for yourself about how you wish to speak English: speaking and writing accurately, or conforming to casual or careless habits.

Bad and Badly

It is obvious that *bad* is an adjective and *badly* is an adverb. However, some native English speakers use *bad* exclusively as both an adjective and an adverb. The problem probably derives from the fact that *bad* seems like an adverb when it follows a linking verb (*to be, to become, to seem, to appear,* etc.):

> That's too bad.
> She looks bad this morning.

You can review linking verbs in Unit 5 on verbs.

You might hear someone say, "That little boy reads and writes *bad.*" However, in this usage an adverb is required. The sentence should be, "That little boy reads and writes *badly.*" Let's look at some examples of how *bad* and *badly* should be used correctly:

You're a bad dog.	(adjective modifying *dog*)
In bad weather we stay at home.	(adjective modifying *weather*)
Your cut isn't so bad.	(adjective following linking verb *is*)
His reply sounded bad.	(adjective following linking verb *sounded*)
You have a badly broken wrist.	(adverb modifying participle *broken*)
They played badly today.	(adverb modifying verb *played*)

Good and Well

This pair of words is misused in much the same way as *bad* and *badly* and for some of the same reasons. But there is extra confusion involved with *good* and *well* because the word *well* can be either an adjective or an adverb, depending upon its usage. *Well* is the adverbial form of *good*, and it is also a word that means *not ill* when used as an adjective.

Good is the opposite of *bad* and is an adjective. Notice how the adjectival and adverbial meanings of this word are used:

Adjective	Adverb
Miguel is a *good* soccer player.	Miguel plays soccer *well*.

If *good* means "kind," you can use *kindly* as its adverbial part:

Adjective	Adverb
David is a *good* man.	He always speaks so *kindly* of them.

But when *well* is used with a linking verb, it is an adjective. You might hear someone say, "I don't feel *good*." That usage is incorrect, for the meaning here is "not ill." The correct usage is "I don't feel *well*."

But that is not the end of the story of *good* and *well*. They both can follow linking verbs, and they both are in that instance considered adjectives. However, their meanings are different:

Sentence with Linking Verb	Meaning
She looks *good*.	She doesn't look bad.
She looks *well*.	She doesn't look ill.
They are *good*.	They aren't bad. **OR** They aren't unkind.
They are *well*.	They aren't ill.

Few and A Few

The difference between the words in this pair is not great. It is correct to say, "Few men are strong enough." You can also say, "A few men are strong enough." But there is a slight difference in implication between the sentences. Let's look at some examples that will demonstrate this difference:

The Sentence	The Implication
Few people saw this movie.	Not many people went to see this movie. (There is a negative implication here.)
A few people saw this movie.	Some people saw this movie but not a lot. (The implication is more positive.)
Few students understood him.	He was hard to understand. (There is a negative implication here.)
A few students understood him.	Some of the students did understand him. (This implication is more positive.)
She has few friends.	She has almost no friends. (There is a negative implication here.)
She has a few friends.	She has some friends but not a lot. (This implication is more positive.)

Use *few* to imply a negative point of view about something. Use *a few* to show a more positive point of view.

Fewer and Less

Many people misuse these two words. But their usage is quite simple: Use *fewer* to modify plural nouns and use *less* to modify singular (and often collective) nouns. *Fewer* is the comparative of *few*, and *less* is the comparative of *little*. Some examples:

Plural Nouns	Singular Nouns
I have fewer books.	I have less money.
We need fewer jobs to do.	She has less time than usual.
Fewer and fewer friends came to visit.	Mom has less and less patience with him.

Now let's compare the *positive* and *comparative* forms of these words:

Positive	Comparative
He has few ideas.	He has fewer ideas than you.
February has few days.	February has fewer days than March.
I have little time.	I have less time now than a year ago.
She has little pain.	She has less pain today than yesterday.

Lay and Lie

Many English speakers confuse these two verbs. *Lay* is a transitive verb and takes a direct object. *Lie* is intransitive and does not take a direct object but is often followed by a prepositional phrase showing a location.

He lays the baby on the bed.	(transitive/direct object = baby)
Where did you lay my book?	(transitive/direct object = book)
Hamburg lies on the Elbe River.	(intransitive/prepositional phrase with *on*)
Your coat is lying over the railing.	(intransitive/prepositional phrase with *over*)

Confusion arises between these two verbs because of their conjugations. Compare them in all the tenses and take particular note of the past tense of *to lie*:

	to lay	**to lie**
Present	he lays	he lies
Past	he laid	he lay
Present Perfect	he has laid	he has lain
Past Perfect	he had laid	he had lain
Future	he will lay	he will lie
Future Perfect	he will have laid	he will have lain

If there is any difficulty deciding whether to use *lay* or *lie*, substitute *put* for the verb. If it makes sense, use *lay*. If it doesn't, use *lie*.

He *puts* the baby on the bed. (makes sense) → He *lays* the baby on the bed.
She *puts* on the bed and sleeps. (makes no sense) → She *lies* on the bed and sleeps.

Little and A Little

This pair of words is similar to *few* and *a few*. *Little* has a negative implication. *A little* shows a more positive point of view. Some examples:

The Sentence	**The Implication**
Little is known about him	Not much is known about him. (There is a negative implication here.)
A little is known about him.	Something is known about him but not a lot. (This implication is more positive.)
She does little work.	She doesn't work much. (There is a negative implication here.)
She does a little work.	She does some work but not much. (This implication is more positive.)
He says little.	He doesn't say much. (There is a negative implication here.)
He says a little.	He says something but not much. (This implication is more positive.)

Than and Then

In rapid conversation these words are rarely confused, even though they sound so much alike. But in writing they must be distinguished. *Than* can be used as a preposition or a conjunction and stands between two elements that are being compared: Marisa is taller *than* Anthony. She runs faster *than* you do.

The word *then* has two major functions: (1) it can be used as an adverb and answers the question *when*, or (2) it can be a conjunction and combines two clauses with the meaning "and as a consequence or thereafter." Let's compare these two functions:

Adverb	Conjunction
We were in Mexico then, too.	I found the book then returned to my room.
Then I decided to go to college.	She slapped his face, then she ran down the street.

Who and Whom

These two words are used frequently, and often misused. *Who* is the form used as the subject of a question:

> *Who* sent you?
> *Who* knows the man over there?

Whom is used as a direct object, indirect object, or the object of a preposition:

> direct object → *Whom* did you meet at the party?
> indirect object → (*To*) *Whom* will you give an invitation?
> object of preposition → *With whom* was he sitting?

Refer to Unit 22 on interrogatives for a review of *who* and *whom*.

It is important to remember that many native speakers of English avoid *whom* and use *who* exclusively. Compare these sentences:

Standard English	Casual English
Whom did they arrest?	Who did they arrest?
From whom did you get the gift?	From who did you get the gift? **OR**
	Who did you get the gift from?

When speaking or writing formally, you should use the standard forms of *who* and *whom*. In casual letters or conversation you can be the judge and avoid *whom*.

exercise   25-1

Circle the better of the two boldface words.

1. Today was a very **bad/badly** day at work.

2. The patient isn't doing **good/well** this morning.

3. He's an awful man. **Few/A few** people like him.

4. Tori has known **fewer/less** happiness in her later years.

5. Does your dog always **lay/lie** in that corner?

6. She's very ill, but we still have **little/a little** hope.

7. I believe this knife is sharper **than/then** that one.

8. **Who/Whom** will you invite to dinner?

9. Her ankle is **bad/badly** swollen.

10. The condition of the wall looks **good/well** again.

11. I'm not poor. I have **few/a few** dollars to give him.

12. You know **fewer/less** about her than I do.

13. If you **lay/lie** that on the shirt, you'll wrinkle it.

14. **Little/A little** kindness won't do him any harm.

15. I grabbed an umbrella **than/then** rushed out the door.

16. A long massage always feels **good/well**.

17. I know **fewer/less** men in this club than you.

18. Did you **lay/lie** my new skirt on the ironing board?

19. Why do you treat your pet so **bad/badly**?

20. You think you're smarter **than/then** I am.

exercise   25-2

Rewrite each sentence in standard English.

1. The little boy acted very bad in class today.

   _____

2. Don't you feel good?

   _____

3. Omar has less friends than his brother.

   _____

4. Mom is laying down for a while.

   _____

5. Kris is prettier then Hilda.

   _____

6. Who did you send the letter to?

   _____

7. Were you in Europe than, too?

   _____

8. I laid on the floor and played with the dog.

   _____

9. Johnny plays good with the other children.

   _____

10. Her voice sounds badly today.

    _____

exercise   25-3

Using the words in parentheses, write original sentences in standard English.

1. (bad) _____

2. (badly) _____

3. (good) _____

4. (well) _____

5. (few) _____

6. (a few) _____

7. (fewer) _____

8. (less) _____

9. (to lay) _____

10. (to lie) _____

11. (little) _____

12. (a little) _____

13. (than) _____

14. (then) _____

15. (who) _____

16. (whom) _____

Common Irregular Verbs

Present Tense	Past Tense	Past Participle
am, are, is	was, were	been
become	became	become
begin	began	begun
bring	brought	brought
build	built	built
buy	bought	bought
choose	chose	chosen
cost	cost	cost
do	did	done
draw	drew	drawn
drink	drank	drunk
drive	drove	driven
eat	ate	eaten
fall	fell	fallen
feel	felt	felt
find	found	found
fly	flew	flown
forget	forgot	forgot, forgotten
get	got	got, gotten
give	gave	given
go	went	gone
grow	grew	grown
have, has	had	had
hear	heard	heard
hide	hid	hidden
hold	held	held
hurt	hurt	hurt
keep	kept	kept
know	knew	known
leave	left	left
let	let	let
light	lit, lighted	lit, lighted
lose	lost	lost
make	made	made
mean	meant	meant
pay	paid	paid
put	put	put
read	read	read

Present Tense	Past Tense	Past Participle
ride	rode	ridden
run	ran	run
say	said	said
see	saw	seen
sell	sold	sold
send	sent	sent
show	showed	shown
sing	sang	sung
sit	sat	sat
sleep	slept	slept
speak	spoke	spoken
stand	stood	stood
swim	swam	swum
take	took	taken
teach	taught	taught
tell	told	told
think	thought	thought
throw	threw	thrown
understand	understood	understood
wear	wore	worn
win	won	won
write	wrote	written

Answer Key

Unit 1 Nouns

1-1
1. proper
2. common
3. proper
4. proper
5. common
6. common
7. proper
8. common
9. proper
10. common

1-2
1. glass
2. Rocky Mountains
3. Mexico
4. flowers
5. bus
6. the store
7. New York Times
8. Roberto
9. Professor Romano
10. my books

1-3
1. direct object
2. subject
3. direct object
4. predicate noun
5. indirect object
6. indirect object
7. subject
8. predicate noun
9. direct object
10. direct object

1-4
Sample Answers:
1. He likes my sister.
2. I want a new car.
3. Did you meet Jackie?
4. I gave the children some candy.
5. I fed a puppy some meat.
6. He sent Grandfather a gift.

1-5
1. The girl does not trust the boys.
2. Father often misplaces his wallet.
3. She always gives the landlord the rent money.
4. Anita wants to sell her new computer soon.
5. She buys her grandchildren the toys.
6. You must visit Ms. Johnson in New York.
7. They like their new house so much.
8. She can give little Johnny the present.
9. He needs to see Dr. Lee today.
10. She throws Michael the ball.

Unit 2 Definite and Indefinite Articles

2-1
1. a
2. the
3. a
4. the
5. —
6. the **OR** an
7. the
8. The **OR** A
9. the
10. a

2-2
1. They gave us oranges.
2. I like the books very much.
3. Do you often visit the farms there?
4. Rabbits are hiding behind it.
5. Katrina likes to play with the kittens.
6. Montel has a dog and a cat.
7. I want to buy the rose.
8. There is a gift for you
9. Can you hear the baby crying?
10. Do you have a brother or a sister?

Unit 3 Adjectives

3-1
1. late
2. little
3. young
4. fast
5. funny
6. handsome
7. early
8. terrible
9. white
10. short

3-2
1. The song from Mexico was sad.
2. The story about a clown is funny.
3. The waiter out of work is careless.
4. The snake from Egypt is ugly.
5. The woman from Spain is beautiful.

3-3
Sample Answers:
1. beautiful
2. chocolate
3. interesting
4. young
5. good
6. old . . . thick
7. new
8. difficult
9. little
10. strange

Unit 4 Personal Pronouns

4-1
1. you
2. him
3. She
4. it
5. me
6. us
7. We
8. they
9. us
10. them
11. you
12. I
13. it
14. us
15. her

4-2
1. They
2. it
3. us
4. they
5. She
6. her
7. They
8. it
9. him
10. it

4-3
Sample Answers:
1. My friend and I
2. the music
3. the books
4. My aunt
5. Craig
6. the teacher
7. the girls
8. The radio
9. Elizabeth
10. the members

4-4

1. I sent it to my friends.
2. She is giving them to us.
3. Trey sold it to her.
4. I didn't buy it for Ella.
5. My brother will bring them to me.

4-5

1. me
2. you
3. him
4. her
5. it
6. us
7. them
8. us
9. us
10. him

4-6

1. it
2. them
3. it
4. her
5. him
6. us
7. them

Unit 5 Verbs

5-1

1. transitive
2. intransitive
3. transitive
4. linking
5. linking
6. transitive
7. intransitive
8. transitive
9. linking
10. transitive

5-2

1. You rarely find a good book./He rarely finds a good book.
2. She often makes mistakes./They often make mistakes.
3. We go home early./I go home early.
4. They can help us./He can help us.
5. She does the dishes./You do the dishes.
6. They must work tomorrow./He must work tomorrow.
7. I borrow some money./She borrows some money.
8. You send a few postcards./We send a few postcards.
9. He can spend the night here./They can spend the night here.
10. They grow very slowly./He grows very slowly.

5-3

1. She has no money./We have no money.
2. He is my cousin./You are my cousin.
3. I am very sick./She is very sick.
4. They have a new car./He has a new car.
5. They are at home now./She is at home now.
6. I am quite well./He is quite well.
7. They have no tickets./She has no tickets.
8. You have a new apartment./He has a new apartment.
9. He is from Costa Rica./I am from Costa Rica.
10. They have a big problem./She has a big problem.

5-4

1. have
2. lives
3. She
4. are
5. It
6. am
7. Are
8. has
9. likes
10. She

5-5
1. Does Rocco's uncle live in Washington?
2. Is she his cousin?
3. Do we take this road to Chicago?
4. Are they in the garden?
5. Do I have your new address?
6. Am I your student? (Are you my student?)
7. Does Linda like Jack?
8. Do you buy flowers every day?
9. Does she sing beautifully?
10. Is it a nice day?

5-6
1. The boys are at home.
2. You want this book.
3. She has the money.
4. I am your friend now.
5. He goes there every day.
6. It is in there.
7. You understand English.
8. The boy feels better.
9. You are in the garden.
10. We have enough money.

5-7
1. Delores is not in the capital.
2. We do not have enough money now.
3. My father does not send him a postcard.
4. The books are not on the table.
5. I do not go home late.
6. I am not an American.
7. The girls do not buy some ice cream.
8. We do not do our homework.
9. Lisa does not like my cousin.
10. It does not seem very old.

5-8
1. Do you not have the time?
2. Does Mike not like this book?
3. Is Kent not at home?
4. Does he not go there every day?
5. Are the girls not happy?
6. Does Sean not speak Spanish?
7. Do the boys not make a cake for her?
8. Do they not do this very often?
9. Does mother not have enough money?
10. Am I not happy about it?

5-9
1. We always drive to New York.
2. She sometimes speaks quickly.
3. I often work in the garden.
4. The boys frequently play tennis.
5. The women travel abroad every year.
6. Doug usually buys German beer.
7. Michelle always talks on the phone.
8. My brother sometimes sleeps in the living room.
9. They usually cook a roast.
10. His sister helps them every day.

5-10
1. She does understand the problem.
2. We do not go to the movies often.
3. I do like that dress.
4. Mac does not want to sell the old car.
5. Mr. Tyner does not write him a long letter.
6. The boys do work in this factory.

5-11
1. Susan helped her friends.
2. We went to the movies.
3. She was washing the car.
4. My father was in the kitchen.
5. She did not understand you.
6. Were you satisfied?
7. Did you always speak Spanish?
8. The girls were riding on a horse.
9. He caught the ball.
10. They played chess after supper.
11. Someone had my wallet.
12. Did Mr. Ibrahim live here?
13. They were learning a new language.
14. Karen worked in New Orleans.
15. You often made mistakes.

5-12
1. He was writing a letter.
2. My mother was sitting in the garden.
3. Jim was standing next to Alicia.
4. The man was bringing us some fish.
5. We were losing the game.
6. The boys were hurrying home.
7. The dog was burying a bone in the yard.
8. I was having a bad day.
9. They were going to the store.
10. He was staying with an uncle.

5-13
1. Did they make some mistakes?
2. Did Will play a few games of cards?
3. Did the girls see the comet?
4. Did her aunt carry the basket into the kitchen?
5. Were they in the city all day?
6. Did Garth learn a good lesson?
7. Was she home all day?
8. Did Robert have the radio?
9. Did the woman run for the bus?
10. Did the dogs fight over a bone?

5-14
1. Lana has been speaking with him.
2. Has he been going to his class?
3. I have been working all day.
4. The tourists have been flying around the world.
5. My parents have been walking along the river.
6. Has the boy been putting his toys away?
7. She has been teaching us all that she knows.

5-15
1. Ms. Nellum has taken the boy home.
2. We have ridden on a bus.
3. They have been riding their bikes.
4. Have you often made cookies?
5. She has not understood.
6. They have been doing their homework.
7. I have been going to the same class.
8. He often has broken his bat.
9. They have been breaking windows.
10. Juanita has written her a letter.

5-16
1. borrowed
2. been
3. Has
4. has
5. listening
6. been
7. been
8. They
9. hurrying
10. written

5-17
1. Julio had written him a few letters.
2. I had been writing a novel.
3. Had you seen a doctor?
4. She had cut her finger.
5. The girls had stayed home again.

5-18
1. The woman had taken the girl home.
2. We had ridden on a train.
3. I had always spoken Spanish.
4. Had you often made roast beef?
5. Rebecca had not remembered.
6. Had he been doing his best?
7. I had been going to the movies.
8. Cindy had taught us English.
9. We had played the same game.
10. Bethany had written in her diary.

5-19
1. The girls will play soccer.
2. I will be learning to drive.
3. We will not be home on time.
4. Will you recognize him?
5. Trent will be driving to Texas.
6. The men will work many hours.
7. She will fly to London every year.
8. Dr. Saloff will not treat her asthma.
9. The little boy will lose his place.
10. Will he be going to the university?

5-20
1. My father will have taken the girl to school.
2. We will have ridden on the subway.
3. They will have been riding their bikes.
4. Will you have made candy?
5. She will not have understood.
6. Will they have done the work?
7. I will have been going to the same class.
8. Chet will have broken his finger.
9. She will have arrived by ten.
10. Sabrina will have written several notes.

5-21
1. Sig bought a car./Sig has bought a car./Sig had bought a car./Sig will buy a car./Sig will have bought a car.
2. I was helping them./I have been helping them./I had been helping them./I will be helping them./I will have been helping them.
3. We came home late./We have come home late./We had come home late./We will come home late./We will have come home late.

5-22
1. Bill is going to take a class at the university./Bill used to take a class at the university.
2. We are going to travel to Germany./We used to travel to Germany.
3. I am going to have lots of parties./I used to have lots of parties.
4. Are you going to live in Ecuador?/Did you used to live in Ecuador?
5. The children are going to watch television every evening./The children used to watch television every evening.
6. Is she going to spend a lot of money?/Did she used to spend a lot of money?
7. They were going to sell the old SUV.
8. Liz was going to begin her studies at the university.
9. The twins were going to live together in San Francisco.
10. Was the attorney going to find a new witness?

Unit 6 Auxiliary Verbs

6-1
1. Serena can buy a new car./Serena wants to buy a new car.
2. We can borrow some money./We want to borrow some money.
3. I can leave at ten o'clock./I want to leave at ten o'clock.
4. The boys can have cereal for breakfast./The boys want to have cereal for breakfast.
5. My sister can be home by 6:00 P.M./My sister wants to be home by 6:00 P.M.
6. They can travel to California./They want to travel to California.
7. Mr. Gutierrez can carry the groceries for her./Mr. Gutierrez wants to carry the groceries for her.

6-2
1. You stay in bed all day.
2. I try hard.
3. My brother is a little late.
4. We find a room for the night.
5. Ms. Brown gets out of bed today.
6. Ramon remains at home today.
7. They learn to behave well.
8. Do you hear me?
9. His girlfriend sells her condo.
10. Do you work every day?

6-3
1. Mr. Weston has to drive to Arizona.
2. We needed to borrow some tools from him.
3. I wanted to leave for Mexico on the tenth of May.
4. Ms. McAdam will be able to help you.
5. Jolene ought to repair the car.
6. Could you understand them? **OR** Were you able to understand them?
7. Aaron was supposed to work on Saturday.
8. She must order the cake today.
9. Have you been able to fill out the application?
10. Our neighbors will want to paint their house.

Unit 7 Passive Voice

7-1
1. Glenda is being kissed by Stuart.
2. She was being spoiled by her parents.
3. My eyes are being tested in the clinic.
4. They were being arrested for a crime.
5. Monique is being awarded a medal.
6. The treasure was being buried on an island.
7. The dog is being punished again.
8. Was the old barn being burned down?

7-2
1. We have been punished by Father.
2. The men have been taken prisoner.
3. She has been thanked by the happy tourists.
4. I have been beaten by a robber.
5. The car has not been washed again.
6. Tony has been examined by the doctor.
7. They have been surrounded by the enemy.
8. Has your sister been fired from her job?
9. Has the baby been carried to his bedroom?
10. She has been congratulated by her boss.

7-3
1. The cottage was destroyed by a storm.
2. Was the New World discovered by Columbus?
3. Our house will be bought by them.
4. The cakes have been baked by my grandmother.
5. The bread is being cut by Phil.
6. The newspapers were being sold by Sergio.
7. Has the money been taken by Iris?
8. The baby will be kissed by her.
9. Is the fence being built by Max?
10. The map was forgotten by her brother.

Unit 8 Subjunctive Mood

8-1
1. She demands Forrest return home by 5:00 P.M.
2. The man suggests you wear a shirt and tie to work.
3. They requested I be a little more helpful.
4. My father demanded we pay for the damage to the car.
5. Did he suggest she come in for an interview?
6. Roger demands that the boy have enough to eat.
7. Did Mother request that her will be read aloud?
8. He has suggested that we be trained for other jobs.
9. Who demanded that the statue be erected on this site?
10. Did he suggest the mayor find a new assistant?

8-2
Sample Answers:
1. . . . she be on time.
2. . . . you stay here tonight.
3. . . . I help him out.
4. . . . he behave himself.
5. . . . he forget about this?

8-3

1. I wish Becca were here today.
2. I wish we were having a big party for Grandmother.
3. I wish he had enough money to buy a condo.
4. I wish my friends had come for a visit.
5. I wish Darnell didn't need an operation.
6. I wish his uncle drove slowly.
7. I wish I could borrow some money from you.
8. I wish the weather were not so rainy.
9. I wish they helped me every day.
10. I wish she wanted to go on vacation with me.

8-4

1. . . . Garrett would ask her out.
2. . . . I would go to the store.
3. . . . he would hear you.
4. . . . I would turn on the heat.
5. . . . he would help me wash the car.
6. . . . it were Erin's birthday.
7. . . . he liked the neighborhood.
8. . . . someone had a soccer ball.
9. . . . I lived in Puerto Rico.
10. . . . the baby were sick.

8-5

1. She would have sold me her bicycle if she had bought a new one.
2. If you had come early, you would have met my cousin.
3. If only Karen had been here.
4. The children would have played in the yard if it had not been raining.
5. If the lawyer had found the document, he would have won this case.
6. If only my mother had been able to walk again.
7. Juanita would have traveled to New York if she had gotten the job.
8. If he had found the wallet, he would have given it to Rick.
9. Jackie would have wanted to come along if he had had more time.
10. If only they had understood the problem.

Unit 9 Adverbs

9-1

1. walked timidly
2. quietly sat down
3. rather angrily
4. entered the classroom noisily
   OR noisily entered
5. too boring
6. talked harshly
7. followed the pretty girl home
8. very smart
9. plays the piano well
10. coldly stared

9-2

Sample Answers:
1. He very neatly stacked the books on the shelf.
2. You sing well.
3. She spoke sadly about the tragedy.
4. You're too weak.
5. He said it rather quickly.
6. I was there yesterday.
7. She never lied to me.
8. The man expressed his beliefs quite strongly.
9. You wrote that too carelessly.
10. She played the song so beautifully.

Unit 10 Contractions

10-1

1. You've
2. I'm
3. He'd
4. They're
5. It's
6. She'll
7. Who's
8. He's
9. We've
10. I'll
11. She's
12. Who'd
13. You're
14. They've
15. It's

10-2

1. mustn't
2. can't
3. won't
4. couldn't
5. aren't
6. Didn't
7. wasn't
8. don't
9. Isn't
10. shouldn't

10-3

Sample Answers:
1. He hasn't left for work yet.
2. You mustn't do that.
3. I shouldn't help you.
4. You needn't be so rude.
5. Weren't you at the game yesterday?
6. I've been here a long time.
7. He'll help us.
8. They're very good friends.
9. You'd like my brother.
10. She's quite ill again.

Unit 11 Plurals

11-1

1. houses
2. wives
3. oxen
4. foxes
5. teeth
6. mice
7. fezzes
8. persons/people
9. candies
10. vetoes
11. deer
12. factories
13. leaves
14. universities
15. juries

11-2

1. The boys are chasing the little mice.
2. His brothers are putting the pots in the boxes.
3. Do the teachers know the men?
4. The heroes of the stories were children.
5. My friends want to buy the knives, spoons, and dishes.
6. Geese are flying over the fields.
7. The clumsy persons/people hurt my feet.
8. The poor women have broken teeth.
9. We saw wild oxen in the zoos.
10. The ugly witches wanted the trained wolves.

Unit 12 Punctuation

1. She took a book from the shelf and began to read.
2. Do you like living in California?
3. She asked me if I know her brother.
4. Sit down and make yourself comfortable.
5. Shut up!
6. How many years were you in the army?

7. I can't believe it's storming again! **OR** .
8. When did they arrive?
9. Watch out!
10. Her little brother is about eight years old.

12-2

1. Ms. Muti, please have a seat in my office.
2. She bought chicken, ham, bread, and butter.
3. By the way, your mother called about an hour ago.
4. Paul was born on May 2, 1989, and Caroline was born on June 5, 1989.
5. No, you may not go to the movies with Rich!
6. Well, that was an interesting discussion.
7. The men sat on one side, and the women sat on the other.
8. Oh, the dress, hat, and gloves look beautiful on you, Jane.
9. It happened on April 5, 1999.
10. Yes, I have a suitcase and flight bag with me.

12-3

1. There are some things you need for this recipe: sugar, salt, and flour.
2. She understood the meaning of the story: Thou shalt not kill.
3. Peter is an excellent swimmer; he coaches a team at our pool.
4. This document is important; it will prove his innocence.
5. Add these names to the list: Irena, Helen, Jaime, and Grace.

12-4

1. She asked, "Why do you spend so much money?"
2. I learned that from "Tips for Dining Out" in a restaurant magazine.
3. Rafael said, "Elena's grandfather is very ill."
4. "This is going to be a big problem," he said sadly.
5. Kurt will say, "I already read 'The Ransom of Red Chief' in school."

12-5

1. The geese's eggs are well hidden.
2. She can't understand you.
3. Is Mr. Hancock's daughter still in college?
4. The two girls' performance was very bad.
5. Ms. Yonan's aunt still lives in Mexico.
6. She met several M.D.'s at the party.
7. Do you know Mr. Richards?
8. The women's purses were all stolen.
9. He won't join the other Ph.D.'s in their discussion.
10. It isn't right to take another man's possessions.

12-6

1. Blake, will you please try to understand my problem?
2. They went to England, Wales, and Scotland.
3. Someone stole my money! **OR** .
4. She asked, "When is the train supposed to arrive?"
5. Mr. Wilson's son wants to buy a house in Wisconsin.
6. I have the following documents: a will, a passport, and a visa.
7. Grandmother died September 11, 1999.
8. Jack is a pilot; he flies around the world.
9. Well, I can't believe you came home on time.
10. Are you planning another vacation?

Unit 13 Infinitives and Gerunds

13-1
1. adverb
2. noun
3. adjective
4. adverb
5. noun

13-2
1. adjective
2. verb
3. adjective
4. noun
5. noun
6. noun
7. adjective
8. verb
9. noun
10. noun

Unit 14 Relative Pronouns

14-1
1. I found the money that belonged to Jack.
2. She has a good memory that always serves her well.
3. This is the woman that I told you about.
4. I have a document that proves my innocence.
5. They want to visit the country that Marsha comes from.
6. This is the doctor who saved my life.
7. Do you know the musician whom I met in Hawaii?
8. She likes the gentleman whom I was telling her about. **OR** She likes the gentleman about whom I was telling her.
9. I visited the sisters whose father had recently died.
10. Jerod noticed the stranger at whom all the neighbors were staring. **OR** Jerod noticed the stranger whom all the neighbors were staring at.
11. Pablo threw away the picture which the boys had found.
12. I live in the house in which my grandfather was born.
13. He bought a suit which is navy blue.
14. Anna has a new hat which I like very much.
15. He wanted to paint the bench on which a man was sitting. **OR** He wanted to paint the bench which a man was sitting on.

14-2
Sample Answers:
1. . . . about whom they wrote so much.
2. . . . that is located in Asia.
3. . . . whom you invited.
4. . . . in which I placed the eggs?
5. . . . that was so funny.
6. . . . whom you told me about.
7. . . . whose book was published.
8. . . . whom my uncle had worked for.
9. . . . blouse that has dark purple buttons.
10. . . . whose passports were lost.

14-3
1. He was in the city I visited last year.
2. Did you finally meet the woman I was telling you about?
3. Ron sold the house he was born in.
4. My father lost the checkbook he kept his credit card in.
5. Did you find the ball I threw over the fence?
6. That's the pretty girl I wrote this poem for.
7. I don't know the people he gave the flowers to.
8. The hat the magician pulled a white rabbit from was empty.
9. She forgot the tickets she had placed next to her briefcase.
10. They live in a tiny village we finally located on a map.

Unit 15 Reflexive Pronouns

15-1

1. You found yourself in a difficult situation./He found himself in a difficult situation./She found herself in a difficult situation./We found ourselves in a difficult situation./They found themselves in a difficult situation./Amy found herself in a difficult situation.
2. I enjoyed myself at the party./You enjoyed yourselves at the party./He enjoyed himself at the party./She enjoyed herself at the party./They enjoyed themselves at the party./The boys enjoyed themselves at the party.
3. I am going to be very proud of myself./My friends are going to be very proud of themselves./Mother is going to be very proud of herself./They are going to be very proud of themselves./We are going to be very proud of ourselves./Abdul and Ricky are going to be very proud of themselves.
4. You just couldn't help yourselves./He just couldn't help himself./She just couldn't help herself. We just couldn't help ourselves. They just couldn't help themselves. The men just couldn't help themselves.

15-2

1. Jerry liked himself in the new suit.
2. They busied themselves with several different tasks.
3. We were very proud of ourselves.
4. She is buying herself a few new outfits.
5. The children hurt themselves.
6. I have to ask myself what to do now.
7. The young woman told herself not to give in.
8. He wants to find himself something nice to wear.
9. You've harmed no one but yourself (yourselves).
10. The lizard hid itself under a rock.

Unit 16 Possession

16-1

1. the storm's center
2. the victims' condition
3. my classmates' behavior
4. the lab's equipment
5. each man's efforts
6. the animals' many illnesses
7. the young lawyer's documents
8. the roses' scent
9. the little bear cub's mother
10. the town's northern border

Unit 17 Possessive Pronouns

17-1

1. The car on the corner is mine.
2. Was this yours?
3. The invading soldier searched theirs.
4. Did Dee find hers?
5. Ours have lived in Brazil for a long time.
6. His is fair with everyone.
7. These problems are entirely his.
8. I need yours.
9. Mine is going to raise the rent.
10. Theirs made no sense.

17-2

1. The women want to visit their relatives in Europe.
2. She takes her children for a long walk.
3. Do you have your tools in the truck?
4. I sent my address and telephone number to the office.
5. We want ours.
6. The picture fell out of its frame.
7. They spend their time in Canada.
8. Are you selling yours?
9. I left some papers in my apartment.
10. Jose found his wallet under the bed.

17-3
1. your
2. his
3. his
4. theirs
5. mine
6. her
7. ours
8. His
9. its
10. my

Unit 18 Prepositions

18-1
1. The man next to him is a senator.
2. Did they leave after it?
3. Evan was dancing with her.
4. Why did you leave the house without it?
5. Are there washers and dryers in them?
6. Juan had some nice wine for them.
7. The man with her is her new boyfriend.
8. A large bear was coming toward him.
9. The letter from them made me very happy.
10. In spite of all of them, Tonya went on smiling.

18-2
1. is
2. women
3. needs
4. was
5. need
6. has
7. makes
8. need
9. don't
10. captures

Unit 19 Capitalization

19-1
1. John, Cadillac
2. Is, Colonel Brubaker, Governor Dassoff
3. The, March, Buffalo
4. We, Chicago
5. In, Whittier School, St. James Park
6. She, February, E. F. Hutton, New York
7. Ms. Assad, Texas
8. Are, Mr., Mrs. Cermak, Britney
9. Ted, Coke
10. The, *The Adventures, Huckleberry Finn*, May
11. His, May, Cleveland Memorial Hospital
12. Mia, A.M.
13. Do
14. If, Mayor Yamamoto
15. We, *New York Times*, Sunday

19-2
1. May tenth, eighteen sixty-five
2. November eleventh, nineteen eighteen
3. July fourth, seventeen seventy-six
4. December twenty-fourth, two thousand
5. January first, nineteen ninety-nine
6. nine A.M.
7. eleven thirty P.M.
8. six forty-five A.M.
9. seven fifty P.M.
10. eight fifteen A.M.

Unit 20 Comparative and Superlative Forms

20-1

1. This freight train is moving slower. **OR** This freight train is moving more slowly.
2. My younger brother is a mathematician.
3. Where is the older man you told me about?
4. Fanny swims better, but she still cannot dive.
5. Hunter's cold is worse today.
6. They have more to do before the end of the day.
7. I think Robbie is more intelligent.
8. The new employee is more careless about his work.
9. She has more friends in the city.
10. This project is more critical to the success of the company.
11. Clarice just can't speak quieter. **OR** Clarice just can't speak more quietly.
12. We have a bigger house out in the country.
13. Do you think that kind of language is more sinful?
14. The inn is farther down this road.
15. Your friend is more reckless.

20-2

1. Cats run faster than dogs.
2. My brother writes more beautifully than your sister.
3. You learn quicker than I do.
4. Rashad sells more cars than Steven.
5. New York is bigger than Chicago.
6. Ginger dances better than Fred.
7. The lake looks bluer than the sky.
8. Our team plays more capably than your team.
9. The husband seems more jealous than the wife.
10. Mr. Espinosa has less money than Ms. VanDam.

20-3

1. Carlos is the shortest boy in the last row.
2. Paris is the most beautiful.
3. The white stallion runs the fastest.
4. Is Russia the largest country in Europe?
5. Is this the most interesting article?
6. They say that the CEO is the richest.
7. Smoking is the worst for your health.
8. The soprano sings the softest.
9. The vice president spoke the most brilliantly.
10. Is the planet Pluto the farthest?
11. Larry gets up the earliest.
12. She is the most systematic about everything she does.
13. Brian is the cutest boy.
14. Laura plays the violin the best.
15. That book is the most boring.

20-4

1. Melanie is the funniest girl in class.
2. What is the most distant planet?
3. Your handwriting is the worst.
4. The men at the party ate the most.
5. Olive is the smartest of all the girls in school.
6. Mozart composed the most beautiful music.
7. Grandmother baked the most delicious cakes.
8. This pickpocket stole the most wallets.
9. Raj thinks this symphony is the most boring.
10. Janice is my best friend.

20-5
1. My coffee is hotter./My coffee is the hottest.
2. Is this math problem more difficult?/Is this math problem the most difficult?
3. I feel better today./I feel the best today.
4. Life in the jungle is more dangerous./Life in the jungle is the most dangerous.
5. This village is poorer./This village is the poorest.
6. Mr. Hong always has less time./Mr. Hong always has the least time.
7. The choir sang a merrier song./The choir sang the merriest song.
8. She wore a shabbier dress./She wore the shabbiest dress.
9. Bert has more friends./Bert has the most friends.
10. She can speak more calmly about it./She can speak the most calmly about it.

Unit 21 Conjunctions

21-1
1. That's my brother, and the woman next to him is his wife.
2. We ran into the tent, but our clothes were already soaked by the storm.
3. Should we watch TV tonight, or should we go see a movie?
4. She began to cry, for the book ended so sadly.
5. I hurried as fast as I could, but (**OR** yet) I arrived home late as usual.
6. The red car was already sold, so Kim bought the blue one.
7. Our dog likes to play in the yard, but our cat prefers to stay in the house.
8. Milo lives on Oak Street, and his brother lives nearby.
9. Their credit was very poor, but (**OR** yet) they decided to buy a piano anyway.
10. I love the snowy beauty of winter, but I hate the heat of summer.

21-2
1. Neither . . . nor
2. either . . . or
3. both . . . and
4. not only . . . but also
5. Neither . . . nor/Both . . . and
6. both . . . and/neither . . . nor
7. not only . . . but also
8. either . . . or
9. Neither . . . nor/Not only . . . but also
10. Neither . . . nor/Both . . . and

21-3
Sample Answers:
1. She left for home after she graduated from college.
2. When she told another joke, Pedro started to laugh.
3. I won't help you unless you make some effort.
4. Do you know where Stephan put his wallet?
5. Once the kids were in bed, I was able to relax.
6. Chris closed the book before he got to the end.
7. You can stay up late as long as you get up on time tomorrow.
8. While I weeded the garden, he relaxed under a tree.
9. I don't remember if I turned off the coffee pot.
10. Now that they live in the city, they often go to the theater.

21-4
Sample Answers:
1. I like the beach, but the water is cold. She's smart, but she's vain.
2. I'll quit unless you pay me more. We're going home unless the weather gets better.
3. Neither the husband nor the wife understood me. I want neither your time nor your money.
4. Do you know where she lives? I found out where you hid the money.
5. I don't know how you knew that. Tell me how I can fix the car.
6. He is my friend and helps me with everything. Alex is a mechanic, and Minnie is a teacher.
7. She's not only bright but also talented. I not only fell down but also tore my shirt.
8. I fought in the battle, for it was the right thing to do. The children were tired, for they had been busy all day.
9. He has no idea when the movie starts. This dog always knows when it's dinner time.
10. Either you find a job, or you find a new place to live. The songs were either too loud or too soft.

Unit 22 Interrogatives

22-1

1. What kind of dress did Lupita buy?
2. Where is Panama located?
3. What did she want to buy?
4. Where did Kevin decide to go?
5. With whom did Kendall spend a lot of time talking?
6. Why did she start to laugh?
7. How did the man on crutches come down the steps?
8. When did the clock stop?
9. Who has worked for this company for years?
10. Whose husband is a firefighter?
11. Which pair of gloves should she select?
12. How many people are in the room?
13. What breed is this dog?
14. What meant danger?
15. Where is Los Angeles from here?

22-2

1. Nikki's
2. a bug
3. tomorrow
4. a Ford
5. that man
6. six feet
7. a friend
8. near the sea
9. better
10. the ending

22-3

Sample Answers:
1. . . . you said that.
2. . . . speaking at the meeting?
3. . . . problems he has.
4. . . . brought the food to the picnic?
5. . . . do such a thing?
6. . . . you were planning to do.
7. . . . they managed to escape.
8. . . . a car pulled in front of me.
9. . . . did you have to pay for it?
10. . . . is going to help us?

Unit 23 Negation

23-1

1. The boys were not playing basketball at the park./The boys weren't playing basketball at the park.
2. My sister is not a concert pianist./My sister isn't a concert pianist.
3. Are you not well?/Aren't you well?
4. His nephew is not learning Japanese./His nephew isn't learning Japanese.
5. Can they not explain how this happened?/Can't they explain how this happened?
6. The judge did not order him sent to prison./The judge didn't order him sent to prison.
7. We will not be traveling to Spain this summer./We won't be traveling to Spain this summer.
8. Does Mr. Amin not have our lawnmower?/Doesn't Mr. Amin have our lawnmower?
9. My sister does not spend a lot of time in the library./My sister doesn't spend a lot of time in the library.
10. Judith did not understand the situation./Judith didn't understand the situation.

23-2

1. I have had enough time to work on this.
2. Mark gets to work on time.
3. She brought her dog along.
4. Have you ever been to New York City?
5. Lin was speaking with someone.
6. The children cooperate with the substitute teacher.
7. They live somewhere in the city.
8. Could the horse run faster?
9. Marta broke the window.
10. Yes, I like this kind of music.
11. Chase is dancing with someone.
12. Can you find something you need?

13. I have written the proposal for them.
14. Yes, she spends her vacation with us.
15. He got something interesting in the mail.

23-3

Sample Answers:
1. I do not understand.
2. They never help me.
3. No one saw the accident.
4. It's not anywhere to be found.
5. He does not have anything for you.
6. None of your work is correct.
7. He has not ever been in Europe.
8. She bought neither purse.
9. The thief was nowhere to be seen.
10. Uma knows nothing about math.

Unit 24 Numbers

24-1

1. Five plus seven is twelve.
2. Eleven minus six is five.
3. Three hundred forty-five minus two hundred twenty equals one hundred twenty-five.
4. Twenty-two times ten equals two hundred twenty.
5. One hundred times sixty-three is six thousand three hundred.
6. Ten thousand divided by five hundred is two hundred.
7. Eight hundred and eighty times three equals two thousand six hundred and forty.
8. Eighty-eight thousand minus fifty-five thousand is thirty-three thousand.
9. Eleven point five times ten is one hundred fifteen.
10. Ninety-three point three divided by three equals thirty-one point one.

24-2

1. second
2. fourth
3. twenty-first
4. third
5. one hundredth
6. thirtieth
7. fifth
8. tenth
9. one thousandth
10. ninety-ninth
11. first
12. twelfth
13. twenty-fifth
14. eighty-sixth
15. twenty-second

24-3

1. August tenth
2. October twelfth
3. November eleventh
4. February sixteenth, nineteen ninety-nine
5. April first, two thousand two
6. December twenty-fourth
7. July fourth
8. fourteen ninety-two
9. February fourteenth, two thousand four
10. June second

Unit 25 Some Important Contrasts

25-1

1. bad
2. well
3. Few
4. less
5. lie
6. a little
7. than
8. Whom
9. badly
10. good
11. a few
12. less
13. lay
14. A little
15. then
16. good
17. fewer
18. lay
19. badly
20. than

25-2

1. The little boy acted very badly in class today.
2. Don't you feel well?
3. Omar has fewer friends than his brother.
4. Mom is lying down for a while.
5. Kris is prettier than Hilda.
6. To whom did you send the letter?
7. Were you in Europe then, too?
8. I lay on the floor and played with the dog.
9. Johnny plays well with the other children.
10. Her voice sounds bad today.

25-3

Sample Answers:
1. This is a bad situation.
2. They played badly today.
3. She's a very good mother.
4. I don't feel well.
5. I have few reasons to doubt you.
6. We have a few things to discuss.
7. There are fewer boys than girls.
8. She has less time now.
9. I'll lay it on the table.
10. He was lying on the floor.
11. There is so little money left.
12. I have a little time to spare.
13. You're younger than Barry.
14. I got up then took a shower.
15. Who is that stranger?
16. Whom will the boss promote?